Kemple Glass
1945 - 1970

by

John R. Burkholder
D. Thomas O'Connor

© Copyright 1997

The Glass Press, Inc.
dba Antique Publications
Post Office Box 553 • Marietta, Ohio 45750

PB ISBN# 1-57080-009-X   HB ISBN# 1-57080-012-X

DESCRIPTIONS OF COVERS

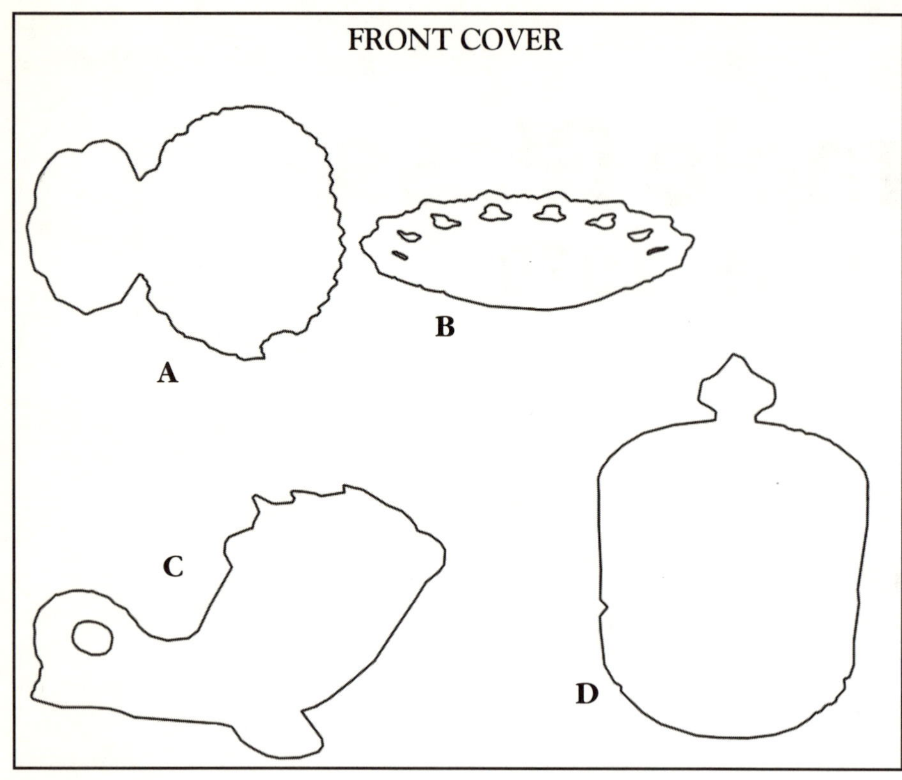

FRONT COVER

A. No. 130 Martec footed jelly or candy, in West Virginia Red.

B. No. 30 Shell & Club 7" plate, open edge, in green.

C. No. 59 Dolphin dish with fish finial cover, in End-of-Day.

D. No. 108 Yutec covered sugar, in milk glass.

E. No. 253 Jumping Horse bookend, in milk glass.

F. No. 251 Deer (Llama) figurine, in milk glass.

G. No. 244 Fighting Cock bookend, in milk glass with red crown.

H. No. 244 Fighting Cock bookend, in amber.

I. No. 253 Jumping Horse bookend, in amethyst.

J. No. 253 Jumping Horse bookend, in amber.

K. No. 251 Deer (Llama) figurine, in amber.

L. No. 252 Pheasant figurine, in amber.

M. No. 255 Grouse figurine, in amber.

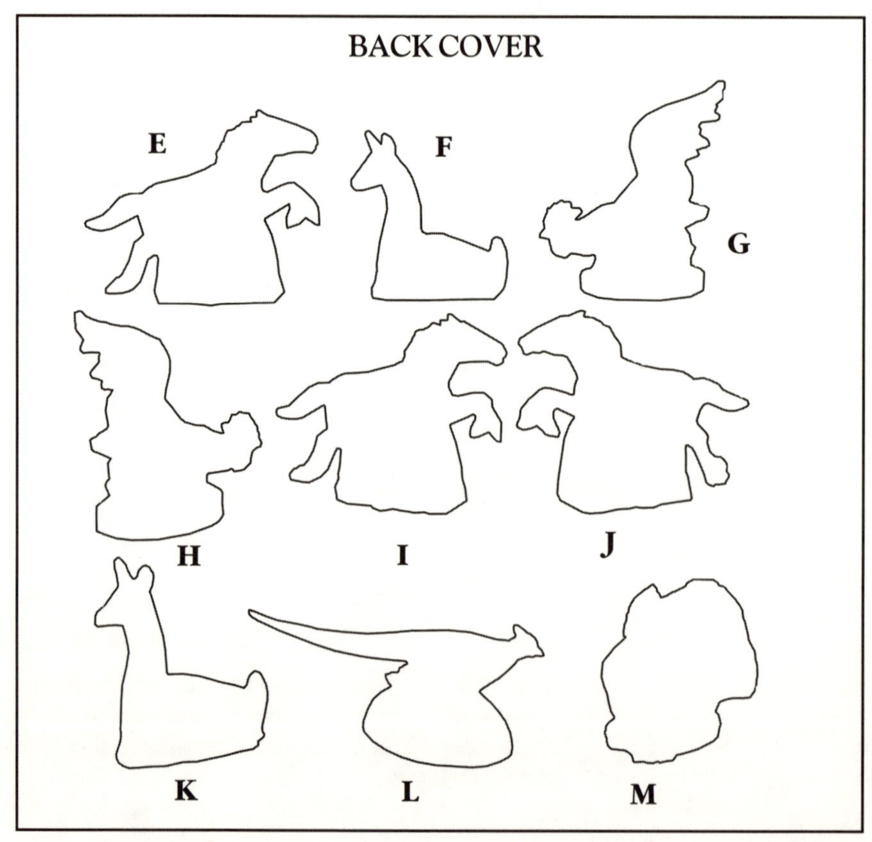

BACK COVER

TABLE OF CONTENTS

FOREWORD

Some projects go quickly from start to finish without a hitch, while others take a slower, more labored course. *Kemple Glass: 1945-1970* certainly fits the second category.

This book had its genesis in the early 1970s. Following the death of John E. Kemple and the closing of the glass works bearing his name, a few individuals wanted to preserve the company's memory and inform collectors about the many beautiful items produced during Kemple's 25-year history. These people were well suited for the task. Everett and Addie Miller had recently self-published two small books on New Martinsville glass. Everett was a successful auctioneer, and he knew about many kinds of American glass. He and his wife, Addie, shared a special interest in Kemple.

Addie's sister, Maxine, was an avid Kemple collector and a close friend of Geraldine Kemple, John's widow and business partner. Maxine and her husband, John Burkholder, had a sizable collection of Kemple glass that would be ideal for illustrating the book.

The Millers and the Burkholders met with Geraldine Kemple on several occasions to gather and verify information. By 1976, Everett and Addie had completed a book draft that was assembled in a three-ring binder. As the time for publication neared, however, some differences arose. As a result, the Millers decided to discontinue the project. Everyone agreed to "sign off" on the proposal, and the book was set aside.

As years passed, the Kemple project was nearly forgotten. Maxine Burkholder passed away even before the Millers had stopped working on the book. Her husband eventually sold a good part of their collection.

In the late 1980s, Everett Miller became ill with cancer. Before his death in 1990, the Millers sold their Kemple catalogs, research notes, and book draft to James Slater, an avid milk glass collector. Slater wasn't sure what he would do with this material, but he felt that it should be preserved.

In the early 1990s, Slater sounded out Antique Publications about printing a book on Kemple glass. The response was favorable. Slater, a retired college professor, was willing to help with the project, but he didn't want the responsibility of authorship.

So Antique Publications contacted John Burkholder about his interest in making the Kemple project a reality. In the intervening years John had remarried. He and his wife, Elsie, liked the book idea at once, as did John's three daughters—Marianne Jones, Carol Justice, and Gerri Stafford. John and Elsie came to Marietta, Ohio, to discuss the details with David Richardson and his staff at Antique Publications.

John had great respect for the glass research of his late brother-in-law, Everett Miller. He knew that the information gathered nearly 20 years ago was still valid. Fortunately, the Burkholders still had a lot of Kemple glass. They also knew where more could be acquired. John agreed to be a co-author with responsibility for providing glass for photography and for being the primary authority on Kemple.

Antique Publications purchased the Kemple material from James Slater and assigned me, as staff editor, the responsibility for writing the text, with assistance from John and his daughters. David Richardson made arrangements for a photography session at the Burkholder home in Logansport, Indiana.

Most of the color photographs for this book were taken by David Richardson in February 1994. Still, the project was delayed, mainly by our company's reorganization and move into new quarters in downtown Marietta, and by my own preoccupation with more immediate assignments.

Finally, in early 1996, the hard work of writing, editing, and organizing resumed in earnest. John Burkholder and I were fortunate to have the cooperation of Geraldine Kemple, who remains mentally alert and full of energy in her mid-90s. Her enthusiasm and persistence were important factors in prompting me to find the needed time to finish this assignment. Although Mrs. Kemple is not responsible for the final form of this book —especially its shortcomings—she did help bring it to birth.

If there is a lesson in telling how this book came to be, it is that worthwhile projects can take a long time to be realized. Perhaps sharing this story will encourage others to complete important tasks that have been long delayed. John Burkholder and I hope that readers of *Kemple Glass: 1945-1970* will find this book "worth the wait."

D. Thomas O'Connor

DEDICATION

This book is dedicated to three individuals who were instrumental in making it a reality:

Geraldine Kemple, supportive wife and active partner in the John E. Kemple Glass Works;

Everett Miller, dedicated glass researcher, now deceased, who prepared a first draft of this book;

Maxine Burkholder, the late wife of co-author John Burkholder and enthusiastic Kemple collector and friend.

In some small way I hope this book will help you, the collector, to know the true story of Kemple. This book is meant to inform you of the reproductions made from the original molds acquired from many sources.

We have tried to make this book as accurate as possible. We hope it will help you in your collecting. May you have as many good times as I have had searching for that hard-to-find addition to your Kemple collection. Happy collecting!

John R. Burkholder

ACKNOWLEDGMENTS

The authors are grateful to many persons who helped to make this book a reality. If anyone has been mistakenly omitted from these acknowledgments, please accept our apology.

We appreciate Geraldine Kemple's cooperation in this project. She provided materials and information that were essential to our efforts.

The late Everett Miller and his wife, Addie, spent many hours gathering and organizing information into a first draft of this book.

The late Maxine Burkholder avidly collected Kemple glass, and she was a good friend of Geraldine Kemple.

James Slater purchased the Kemple research materials from the Millers, and later approached Antique Publications about the possibility of doing this book.

Publisher David Richardson provided ongoing support and encouragement. He also photographed the items shown in the color section.

John Burkholder's three daughters—Marianne Jones, Jerri Stafford, and Carol Justice—assisted their father in preparing the photo captions and value guide, They also reviewed much of the text and made valuable suggestions.

Elsie Burkholder provided encouragement, and was a gracious hostess during visits to the Burkholder home.

Gay LeCleire Taylor, curator of the Museum of American Glass at Wheaton Village (New Jersey), supplied helpful information, as did Beverly Narbut also of Wheaton Village. Virginia Wright of the Rakow Library, Corning Museum of Glass (New York) sent material on microfiche which aided our research.

Robert Shietze and Robert and Angie Beall loaned Kemple pieces for the photography session.

Brady Peery, graphics artist, supplied the initial layout and design for this book.

Terry Richards Nutter, Antique Publications' staff member, supervised the layout, provided technical support, did proofreading, and scanned numerous photos.

Finally, Tarez Samra Graban, associate editor for Antique Publications, was involved in every phase of preparing this book. In addition to writing the first draft of chapters four, six, and seven, she did most of the typesetting and participated in layout decisions. Tarez kept this project moving forward, and she deserves much credit for its completion.

HOW TO USE THIS BOOK

This book can be divided into three parts: (1) a narrative section of seven chapters (pp. 7-46, 113-127); (2) a pictorial section in color (pp. 47-112); and (3) an appendix of catalog reprints, various indexes, and a value guide (pp. 128-160).

The narrative section tells the story of the John E. Kemple Glass Company. After an introductory chapter on the firm's 25-year history, the remaining chapters focus on how molds were acquired from different sources and on the items produced from those molds. The last chapter follows the molds to Wheaton Industries and lists the pieces made by Wheaton after the Kemple Glass Works closed.

Whenever possible, illustrations are placed close to descriptions in the text. Some cross references also appear in parentheses as patterns are introduced. This enables the reader to find a page on which the pattern is pictured.

Scores of patterns and items are presented as succinctly as possible, which makes for "dense reading" in places. Readers are not expected to absorb everything in one sitting. After perusing the narrative section, it might be helpful to study the illustrations in the color pages, then return to the narrative for a more careful reading.

The first part of the color section includes 796 numbered pieces, mostly from John Burkholder's collection. Items are often grouped by categories—type of ware, pattern, color, etc.—but some pages show miscellaneous assortments. We have made the pictures as large as possible, while still allowing for captions on each page. The captions give ware (or item) numbers and descriptions as they appeared in Kemple catalogs or price lists.

The second part of the color section features Kemple and Wheaton catalog reprints. If Kemple ware numbers appear in the catalog picture, the index on p. 137 will allow the reader to identify these pieces. The value guide for this section also uses these ware numbers. On pp. 106-107, letters and numbers have been added to the pictures so that we can identify these items for the value guide.

The last section of this book includes additional catalog reprints in black and white, indexes by product number and pattern name, a value guide, and a bibliography. In a very few cases, the product number or pattern name is either uncertain or unknown. The indexes enable the reader to find a specific pattern or item with a minimum of page turning.

CHAPTER ONE
THE KEMPLE STORY

The John E. Kemple Glass Works would never have existed were it not for a chance meeting on a bus. John Kemple noticed a pretty fellow passenger and asked the driver who she was. Not long afterwards, the two were introduced by a mutual friend and they began dating.

It was the early years of World War II. John was an experienced glass artisan, the fifth generation in a family of glass makers. Divorced and a bit down on his luck, he was working part-time as a street car conductor. Geraldine, the mother of two grown boys, was also recovering from a broken marriage. She had worked in advertising and as a sales clerk, once helping to organize a retail clerk's union.

At the time she met John, Geraldine owned a gift shop. Her business was booming with the growing popularity of greeting cards. Geraldine also had an artistic flair, and she decorated ceramics for sale in her shop.

Soon after John and Geraldine married in 1941, they began to think about starting a glass company. Each had the experience necessary for a successful partnership. John knew glass making inside and out, having begun as an 11-year-old at the Fostoria plant in Moundsville, West Virginia. For her part, Geraldine had a head for business, and she was a hard worker. Their plans were realized in May 1945 when they leased two large adjoining buildings in East Palestine, Ohio. Geraldine sold her gift shop to help finance the operation.

One of the keys to the Kemples' success was their ability to acquire excellent glass molds. A few of these old molds dated to 1840, but most came from the 1870-1900 era. Before they started making glass, the Kemples purchased 246 hand-press molds from the Mannington Art Glass Company of West Virginia. Most were for novelty items such as plates, stamp boxes, pomade jars, pin trays, powder boxes, and soap dishes. Many origi-

Geraldine and John Kemple at an early Pittsburgh trade show.

John E. Kemple (circa 1950s).

Geraldine R. Kemple in the sales room.

nated from the Gillinder and Dithridge glass companies.

Additional molds were acquired over the years until Kemple owned more than 1,100. From Tuska, a New York distributor, they bought molds in Lace and Dewdrop, Ivy-in-Snow, Blackberry, and Moon and Star Variant. From American Art Glass came the Fighting Cock, the Church Lamp, and Haley's Compote. A large number of molds came from the McKee Glass Company. Most important of these were the covered animal dishes with split rib and basketweave bases (many marked with a "K") and the various Prescut "Tec" patterns (Aztec, Bontec, etc.).

During its 25-year history (1945-1970), Kemple Glass specialized in "Authentic Antique Reproductions." Even collectors who despise the word "reproduction" have to admit that the Kemples ran an honest business with the old molds they purchased from defunct glassworks such as Mannington and McKee.

At first, Kemple made only milk glass in molds used mainly for clear glass in the Victorian era. In 1960, colored wares were added to the Kemple's line. Glass was marked by stickers and, whenever practical, a "K" was added to the molds. Although Kemple made some blown wares, mostly they produced pressed glass for gift shops and department stores—items that should not confuse knowledgeable collectors of Victorian pattern glass. In so doing, Kemple gave a new lease on life to hundreds of molds that were too good to rust away in a factory warehouse or be converted into scrap iron.

Although John had primary responsibility for managing the factory, Geraldine was an equal partner right from the start. She would go into the storage areas with John to help select the molds. Taking a hands-on approach, she was not afraid to mix glass batches and assist at the furnace. Whatever needed to be done, from packing glass to keeping the books, she did with gusto.

Few people appreciate the amount of time and expense that went into producing a glass mold. Gay LeCleire Taylor, curator at the Museum of American Glass at Wheaton Village, Millville, New Jersey, gave a lecture based on the Kemple molds in their possession. Included was information obtained from the family of Monroe Husted, a mold maker trained in Pittsburgh in the early 1900s. Ms. Taylor explained, "When a mold arrived from the foundry, it had a smooth interior with the desired shape. With lathes, files and chisels, the desired design was carved into the mold." As one example, she stated that "a 6" Aztec butter cover took 226 hours to carve in a three-part mold." She concluded, "When I looked carefully at the mold and thought of Monroe Husted's hard work, I realized that a mold could be a small masterpiece."

In 1949, the trademark "John E. Kemple Glass Works, East Palestine, Ohio," appeared in relief on the bottom of a few plates. Then, beginning in 1950, a "K" was chiseled into some of the molds. As molds were reworked, stippling was also added to bottoms and the inside of lids. The stippling helped to prevent "checks," "crizzles," and other flaws in the glass.

The Kemple Glass Works succeeded almost from the start. Then, in 1956, the factory burned to the ground. The circumstances of the fire were mysterious and arson was suspected. Nevertheless, the buildings' owner collected on the insurance policy.

John and Geraldine had coverage on their equipment and merchandise, but it was not sufficient to meet their losses. Trying to regroup, they leased another glass plant for a few weeks. Then, an opportunity came to buy the old Gill Glass Works in Kenova, West Virginia. The decision was made to move to the neighboring state.

In the years at East Palestine, the Kemples made only white milk glass, except for a small amount of blue milk glass. The quality of this glass was excellent, thanks to a formula that was a jealously guarded Kemple family secret. Throughout the rest of the 1950s at Kenova, the Kemples continued to make and sell milk glass with great success. Then, beginning in 1960, they began adding colored wares to their line. Before the close of the decade, more colored glass was manufactured than milk glass. In all, Kemple Glass was produced in about 20 colors, including West Virginia Red and the multi-hued "End-of-Day."

As the firm grew, Geraldine focused on sales and running the office, while John managed the factory. During the 1960s, tour buses visited the Kemple Glass Works on a regular basis. An outlet store operated in downtown Kenova, some distance from the glass plant. Geraldine was everywhere—leading tours and supervising the office and store employees. John was responsible for the manufacturing end of the business. At its peak, Kemple employed over 50 workers and had jobbers from coast to coast. Although pressed ware was the mainstay, some off-hand creations were made as well. Thousands of pieces of glassware were produced, providing a golden opportunity for today's collectors.

Despite the long hours and demands of the business, the Kemples took pleasure in other pursuits. Together they enjoyed raising several Doberman pinschers as pets. John loved baseball, and for several years the Kemples sponsored a team. Geraldine was quite active in her Methodist church. A news clipping gives us a slice of small-town life from the 1950s: "Employees of the Kemple Glass Works and their families enjoyed a Christmas party Monday evening given by Mr. and Mrs. John Kemple. The program consisted of solos and recitations. . . Mrs. Kemple whistled 'Silent Night' after which group singing of Christmas carols was enjoyed."

Life turned serious around 1967 when John Kemple became ill. The responsibility for running the business fell more and more upon Geraldine. She met this chal-

The *John E. Kemple Glass Works* of East Palestine, Ohio, wishes to announce they have acquired the interests of the Gill Glass Company, Kenova, W. Va. and are in the process of moving their glass factory to this West Virginia city. They expect to be in operation late December. They will manufacture a complete line of *Hand Made Authentic Antique Reproductions in Milk Glass.* Processed in the original old moulds for which the company has been famous for many years. Visitors always welcome as in past years.

A postcard used to inform customers of Kemple Glass Works' move from Ohio to West Virginia.

Early letterhead stationery.

A gatherer brings molten glass to presser Ray Martin.

Mixing the batch.

Ray Martin presses hot molten glass into a mold to create a footed compote.

The John E. Kemple Glass Works factory at East Palestine, Ohio (c. 1950).

John E. Kemple finishing a compote.

Warming-in boy, Dave Yarian, at the glory hole.

Leveling the foot on a compote.

An early advertisement for Kemple's 20-piece milk glass assortment.

Selector Dorothy Vale in the packing department.

A Kemple employee shows the Moon & Star Variant banana boat to a tour of jobbers and salesmen.

An outlet for Kemple Glass wares and gifts in Kenova, West Virginia.

Dorothy Shafernock inspects pieces at the end of the annealing lehr

Geraldine Kemple at age 92.

lenge, as she had others before, while also caring for John the best she could. John died in 1970, and soon thereafter the business was sold. Geraldine was nearly 70, and she began a well-deserved retirement. The following years she remained active in various activities, which included giving talks on Kemple glass to appreciative audiences.

At the time of this writing, Geraldine lives in Ohio at the Canton Christian Home, a residence for seniors. She has a comfortable studio apartment and gets around with help from a walker with wheels on its front legs. Her glass collection has been culled to fit her surroundings, but she has some choice pieces to display. At 95 years of age, Geraldine still has remarkable energy, and she recalls many details from her years in the glass business.

In 1970, the John E. Kemple Glass Works closed its doors. The factory at Kenova, West Virginia stands no more. Most of its well-traveled molds have found a new home at Wheaton Industries in Millville, New Jersey. The company's memory is preserved by milk glass collectors and admirers of colored pattern glass.

CHAPTER TWO

MANNINGTON ART GLASS PURCHASES

The Kemple story is largely a tale of old glass molds that were purchased and restored to use. In 1944, one year before the Kemples began producing glass, they bought about 120 molds from Mr. Picallo, owner of the Mannington Art Glass Company in Mannington, West Virginia. Then, in 1945, the Kemples acquired another 126 molds from this firm.

Gay LeCleire Taylor, curator of the Museum of American Glass, Wheaton Village, Millville, New Jersey, found information on this company while preparing a lecture on the Kemple molds. A 1928 glass directory mentions that Mannington had one furnace with six pots, from which they made milk glass eggs and various novelties. All of the molds sold to the Kemples were in this category. They included plates and other small items, such as stamp boxes, pomade jars, pin trays, powder boxes, cuff link boxes, and soap dishes.

In Everett Miller's original research for this book, he stated: "Records indicate that many of these [Mannington] molds originated from the Gillinder and Dithridge Glass Companies." Miller also indicated that Mannington's milk glass had a cream or gray cast, whereas the eleven-ingredient Kemple formula produced a very white, high quality milk glass.

Several items from the Mannington mold purchase incorporate a "scroll" in the pattern. Examples include an oblong dresser tray and five variously sized boxes in *Scroll with Flower*. The pattern *Scroll Variant* consists of three dresser boxes, three trays, toothpick holders (round, square, and hexagonal), cigar and tobacco jars, matchholder, powder jar, salt dip, and an $8^{1}/_{2}$" plate. Other scroll patterns include *Scroll with Beaded Edge* (salt dip), *Scroll with Fleur de Lis* (covered jewel box, round dresser box, oval tray), *Beaded Scroll* (oval covered dresser box, covered pen box), *Small Scroll* (square-base candlesticks), and *Heavy Scroll* (dresser tray). Many of these scroll patterns are illustrated on pages 12, 16, 18, 19, 60, 97, and 128.

Among the Mannington molds were two attractive floral patterns, *Cabbage Rose* and *Fleur de Lis*. The Cabbage Rose pieces included a mug, oval jewel box, round dresser box, and $7^{1}/_{2}$" x 10" tray. The Fleur de Lis pieces included a low round powder box and a rectangular covered jewel box. These patterns are illustrated on the same pages as the scroll patterns above.

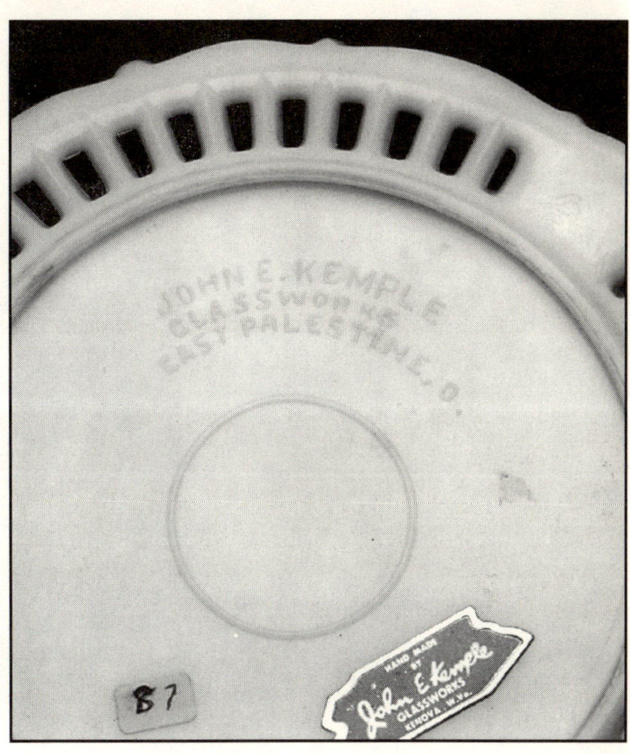

One of the few Mannington plates engraved with the John E. Kemple Glassworks factory identification. Most other pieces had paper labels, and some molds were engraved with the letter "K".

Other early mold purchases from Mannington allowed Kemple to reproduce a variety of Victorian figural novelties. These include: *Waffle Hat* toothpick; *Basket weave* flared toothpick and two-handled *Basket* toothpick; *Pansy Flower* three-handled toothpick; *Indian Chief* toothpick, match holder, and wall match holder; *Coal Bucket with Bail* ash tray; *Heart* ash tray (or pin tray); 5" *Spade* ash tray; 3" *Heart/Spade/Club/Diamond* ash trays; *Horseshoe* ash tray; *Wooden Tub* master salt; *Puss-in-Boots* slipper (one with pointed toe and solid sole, the other with round toe and open sole); *Lady's Boot* vase; *Mary*, *Jesus*, and *Cherub* plaques; *Chick* egg cup; and *Easter eggs* (6" x 5" and 4" x 5"). See pages 16, 19, 56, 61, 62, 74, 91, 92, 103 and 129 for illustrations.

From various Lion molds, the company produced a *Lion Head* 7" x 11" dresser tray, rectangular covered dresser box, and round covered dresser box, as well as a Lion Head pin tray. Candlesticks included a $7^{1}/_{2}$" *Crucifix* with floral bottom and one in the *Narcissus* pattern. Items in the *Versailles* pattern were a rectangular covered

No. 30 Shell and Club decorated plates, 7" and 9$^1/_2$" size.

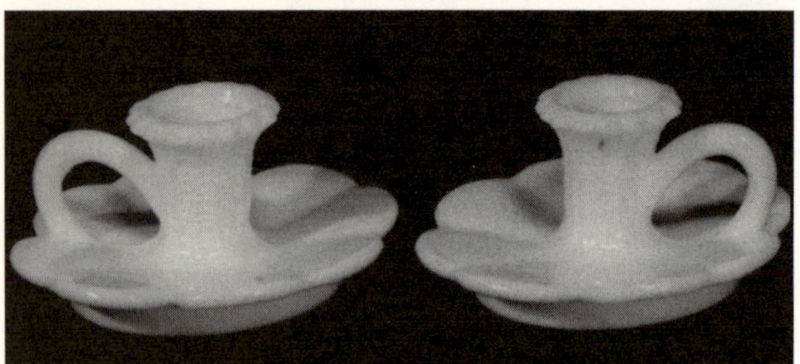

No. 94 Narcissus candlesticks

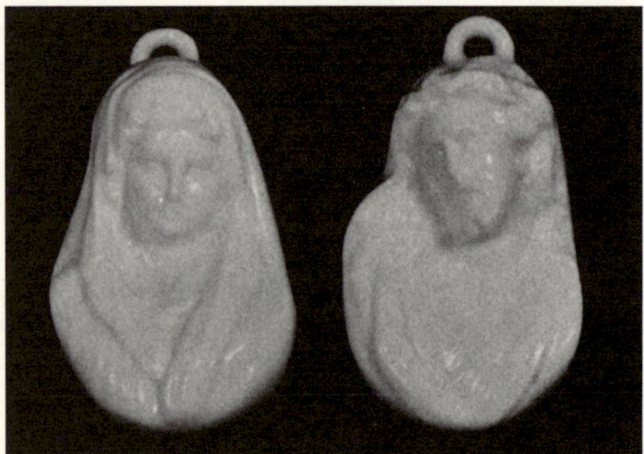

Kemple No. 19-A, B Mary and Jesus plaques.

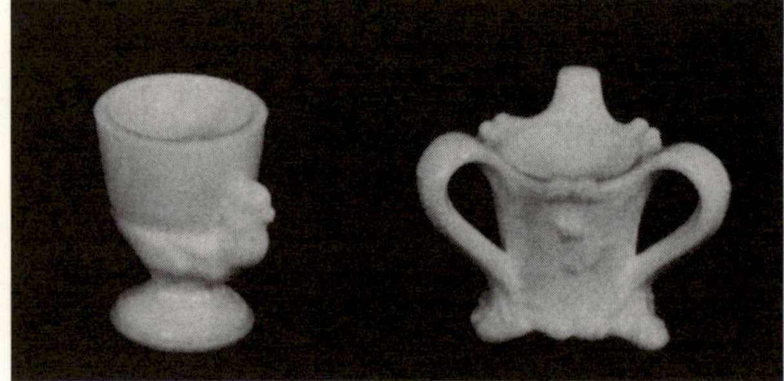

No. 21 Chick egg cup and
No. 5 three-handled Pansy toothpick.

No. 132 Small Scroll square base candlesticks.

From left to right:
No. 43-I Ivy decorated heart pin tray,
No. 3-R Scroll Variant dresser box in Rose decoration,
and No. 18-V Scroll with Flower covered box with Violet.

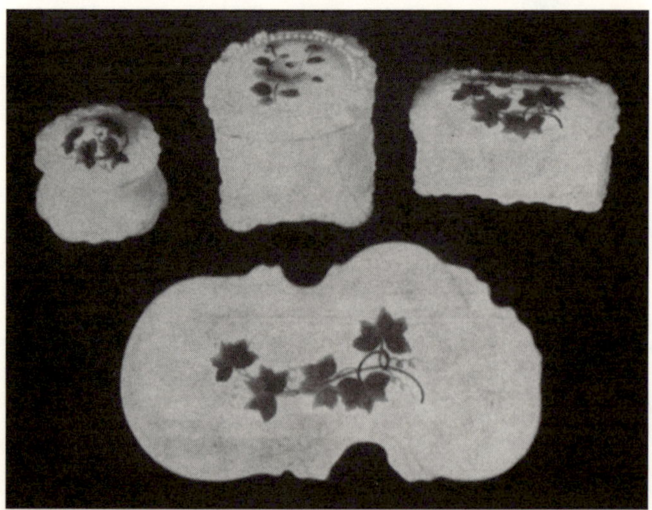

Clockwise from top left: No. 6-I Scroll with Flower collar box painted with Ivy, No. 8-R Cabbage Rose round dresser box, No. 2-I Scroll with Flower rectangular dresser box painted with Ivy, and No. 5-I Scroll with Flower Ivy.

No. 16 7" Panel Peg-Open Edge
and No. 11 6" Lacy Heart plates.

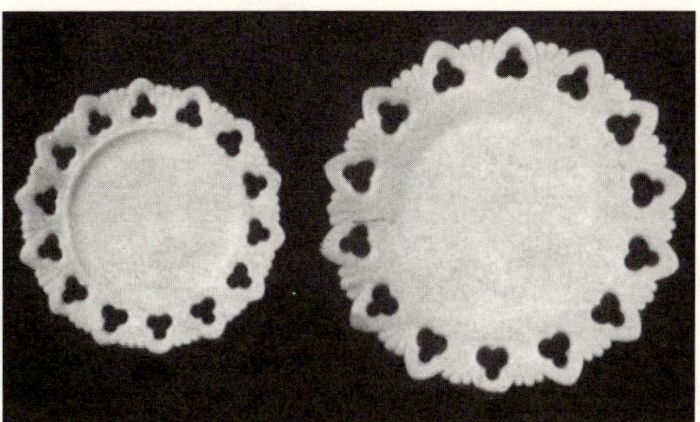

No. 30 7" and No. 38 9½" Shell & Club plates.

No. 17 Lovers' Knot and No. 29 Angel Head plates.

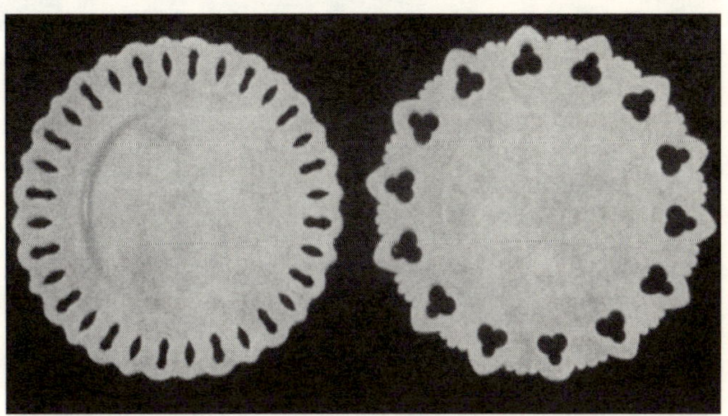

No. 42 8½" 101-Open Edge and
No. 37 9½" Shell & Club with waffle face plates.

No. 16 7" Panel Peg-Open Edge plate in Pear,
Peach, Grape and Plum decoration.

No. 17 Lovers' Knot 8½" plate in Plum,
Grape, Ivy, and Violet decorations.

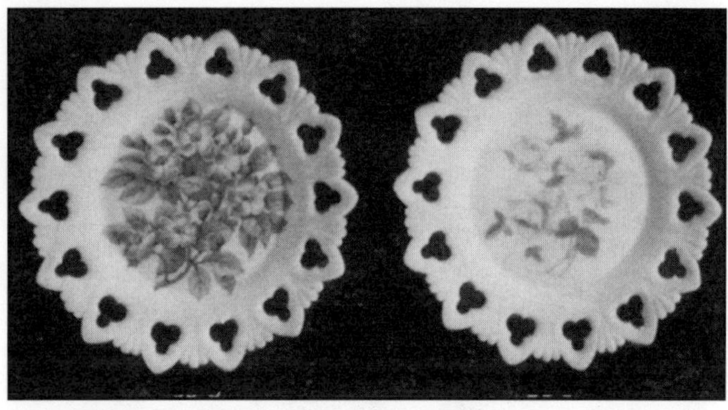

No. 38-D, E 9¹/₂" Shell & Club plates in Apple Blossom and Yellow Rose decorations.

No. 38-B, C 9¹/₂" Shell & Club plates in Antique Rose and Colonial decorations

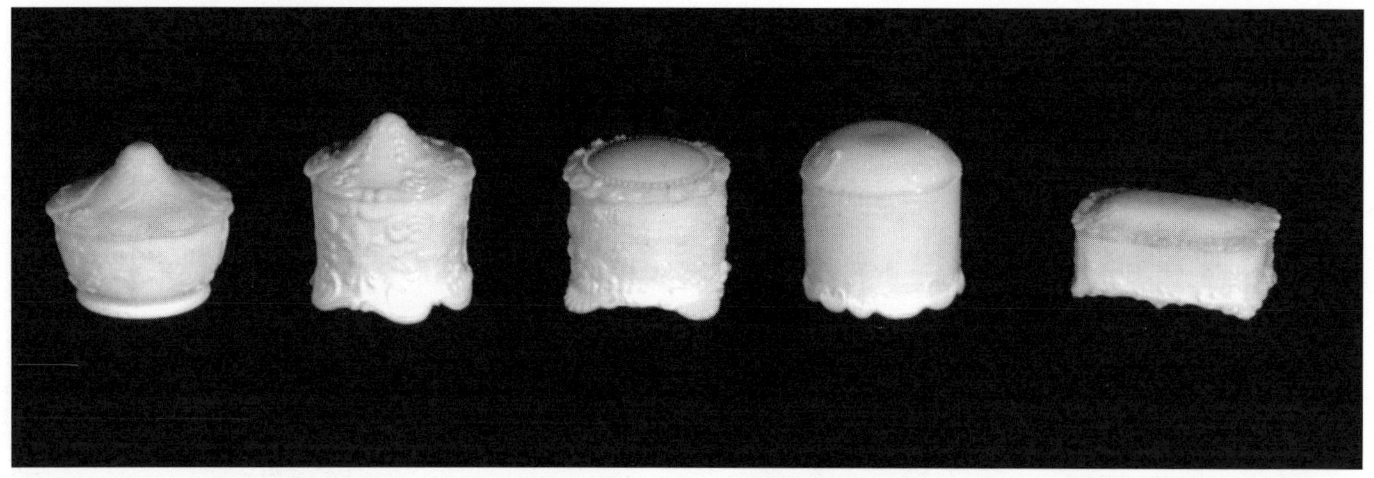

Dresser boxes—No. 12 Fleur de Lis, No. 7 Scroll with Fleur de Lis, No. 8 Cabbage Rose, No. 10 Scroll Variant, and No. 2 Scroll with Flower.

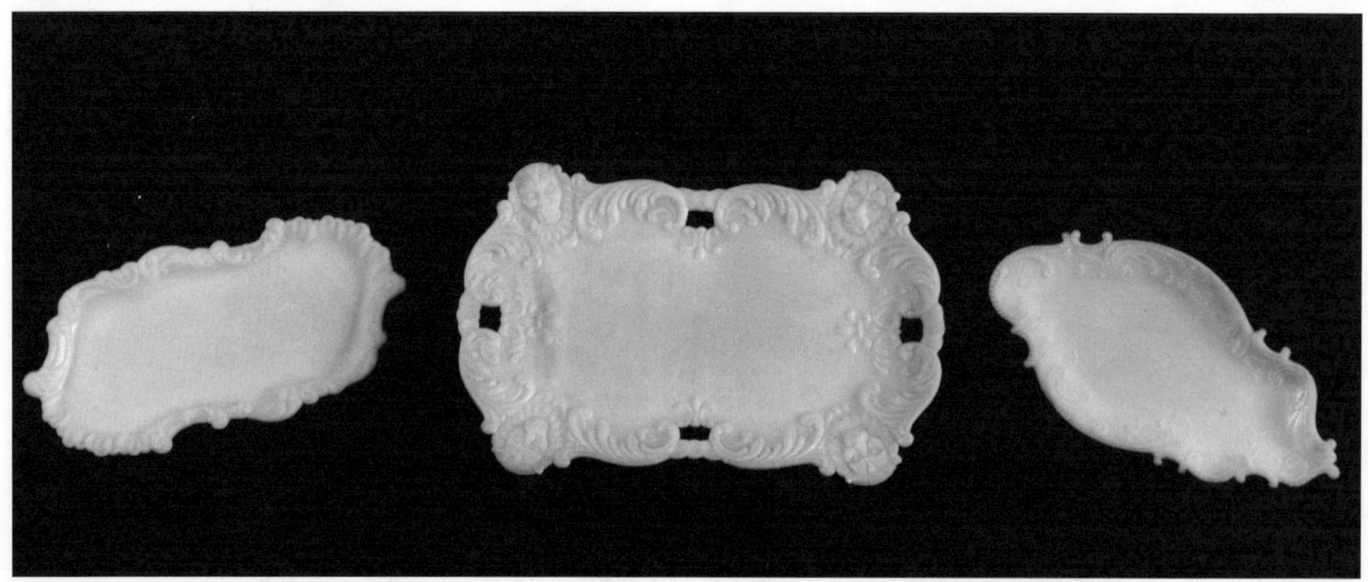

The No. 4 Scroll Variant pin tray (listed in some Kemple catalogs as No. 205), No. 901 7" x 11" Lion Head tray, and No. 199 7" Beaded Swirl pin tray.

No. 162 two-handled Basket
toothpick.

No. 18V Scroll with Flower covered dresser box
in Violet decoration.

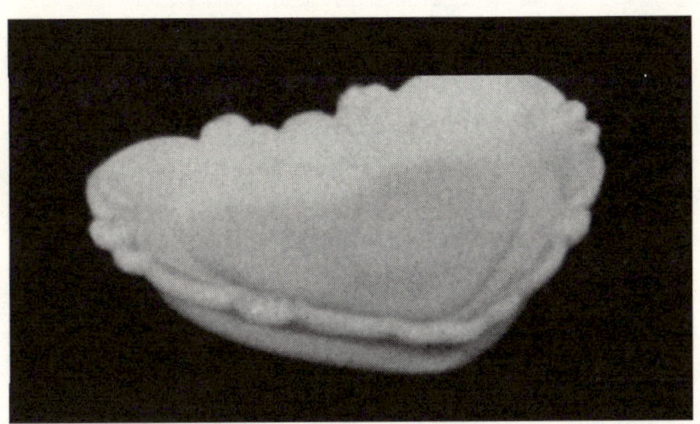

No. 43 Heart pin tray

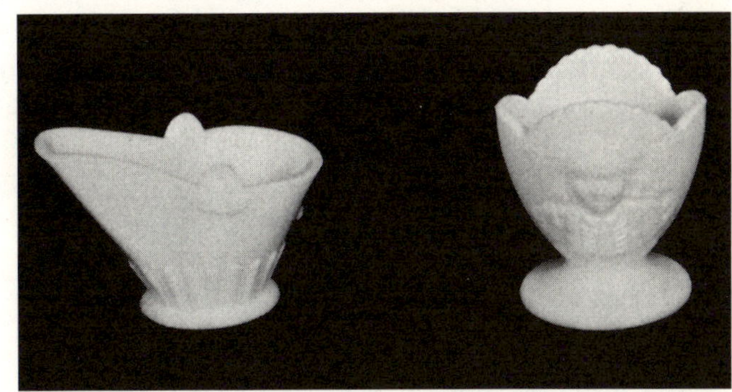

No. 210 Coal Bucket with Bail ash tray
and No. 178 Indian Chief toothpick.

No. 29 Angel Head 8$^{1}/_{2}$" plates in the Lord's Supper,
Mary, and Christ decorations.

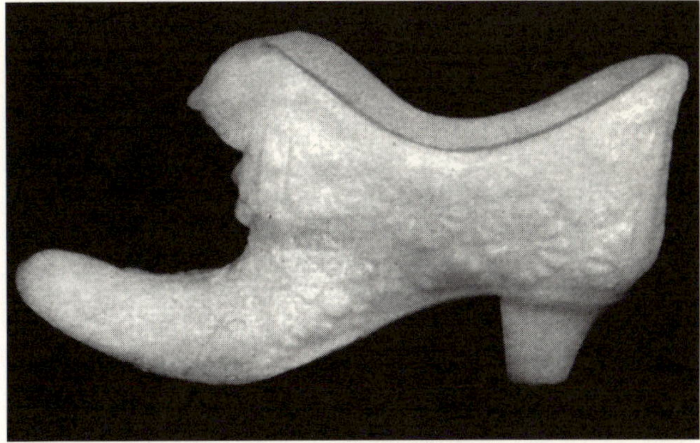

No. 32 Puss-in-Boots Slipper,
pointed toe with solid sole.

An early advertisement for Kemple's item No. 16—decorated Panel Peg-Open Edge plates.

cigarette box, and oval and rectangular covered dresser boxes. Finally, a 7" pin tray was manufactured in the *Beaded Swirl* pattern. Refer to pages 16, 18, 60, and 79 for illustrations of these items.

Plates, both plain and decorated, comprised a significant number of the early Kemple products made from Mannington molds. The patterns included *Sheaf of Wheat* (6½", 7½", 8"), *Lacy Heart* (6", 7½"), *Shell and Club* (7", 9½"—plain and waffle face), *Angel Head* (8½"), *Lovers' Knot* (8½"), *Panel Peg-Open Edge* (7½"), *Panel Peg with No. 54 Candlestick* cake plate, *101-Open Edge* (8½"), *Inverted Heart-Open Edge* (7"), *Maple Leaf-Open Edge* (9"), *Sandwich "Basket"* plate (8"), *Mary and Child* (6"), and *Rose* Pattern, hand-painted. These plates are illustrated on pages 15-19, 49, 50, 63, and 94.

Plate decorations were mostly hand-painted, although decals were used in later years. Some of the early decorating was done by Geraldine Kemple. The designs included flowers, fruit, birds, pastoral scenes, and people. The ad pictured above shows a 12-piece set of 7½" Panel Peg-Open Edge plates, each with a different decoration.

In all, at least 87 different items can be found in Kemple price lists and catalogs that were produced from molds purchased from the Mannington Art Glass Com-

pany. As Kemple acquired molds from other sources, many of the Mannington pieces were dropped from the line. Some, however, continued to be produced off and on throughout the firm's 25-year history.

The 1948 price list has 14 gift specialties made from these molds, including Lacy Heart plates, eight boxes in various Fleur de Lis and Scroll patterns, three trays, and a Cabbage Rose mug. Considerably more Mannington items appear in the 1952 Kemple catalog. In addition to plates in virtually all the patterns and decorations, one finds the Puss-in-Boots slipper, Mary and Jesus plaques, and a large assortment of boxes. In the 1958-1962 catalog, however, only 14 Mannington items are shown, although not the same ones as those in the 1948 price list. Included are plates in Shell & Club and Sheaf of Wheat, the Chick egg cup, Narcissus candlesticks, and Pansy three-handled toothpick holder.

The Kemples were fortunate indeed to acquire so many good molds from the Mannington Art Glass Company. Were it not for these sturdy objects, the John E. Kemple Glass Works wouldn't have been able to make a strong beginning. These various novelties and plate patterns have a timeless appeal and these wares are attractive in milk glass or a variety of colors.

CHAPTER THREE

THE TUSKA PURCHASES

AN ELEMENT OF MYSTERY

In early 1946, the Kemples purchased about 70 well-traveled, hand-press glass molds from H. M. Tuska, a New York distributor. Whereas the molds acquired earlier from Mannington were mainly for small novelty pieces, the Tuska molds enabled the Kemples to produce a variety of tableware items in four well-known patterns: *Lace & Dewdrop* (aka Lacy Dewdrop, Beaded Jewel, Co-Op No. 1902); *Ivy-in-Snow* (aka Ivy and Snow, Forest Ware); *Moon and Star Variant* (aka Imperial, Jeweled Moon and Star); and *Blackberry* (aka Dewberry, Co-Op No. 375—not the Hobbs, Brockunier Blackberry).

Some glass authors state that these molds originated at George Duncan and Sons, Pittsburgh, in the 1870s and '80s (Belknap, *Milk Glass*, p. 270; Ferson, *Yesterday's Milk Glass Today*, p. 151). In this view, the molds were sold to the Co-Operative Flint Glass Company of Beaver Falls, Pennsylvania, about 1902. Then, around 1929, they were sold again—this time to the Phoenix Glass Company in nearby Monaca. At Co-Operative, the molds had been used only to produce clear glass, but Phoenix made a number of milk-glass items. When Tuska acquired them in the early 1940s, he tried, without great success, to have Westmoreland (and possibly other glass companies) produce milk glass in some of these patterns. Then, in 1946, he sold

A Kemple catalogue page displays Lace and Dewdrop variations on two molds, manufactured at the Kenova, West Virginia plant. *Top row:* 8" covered compote, covered butter, covered nut dish with finial. *Bottom row:* 6" open compote, tall covered sugar, water pitcher, and 6" covered compote. Kemple item numbers are shown.

Kemple's most widely produced pattern: Lace & Dewdrop (also called "Beaded Jewel").
Top row: No. 409 36 oz. water pitcher, No. 408 8 oz. goblet, No. 407 tumbler; *Middle row:* No. 406 4" sauce,
No. 404 6" bowl, No. 405 8" bowl; *Bottom row:* No. 422 10" bowl, No. 420 4$^{1}/_{2}$" candlesticks.

the molds to the John E. Kemple Glass Works.

When Everett Miller did research on the Kemple Glass Works 20 years ago, he thought these four patterns could be traced to George Duncan in the 1880s. The Kemples also believed this to be true, perhaps because of what Tuska told them at the time of purchase.

Other glass researchers, however, say that these molds originated at the Co-Operative Flint Glass Company in the late 1890s and early 1900s. This is the position of Albert Christian Revi (*American Pressed Glass and Figure Bottles*, pp. 129, 279); Lowell Innes (*Pittsburgh Glass, 1797-1891*, p. 381); Kenneth M. Wilson (*American Glass, 1790-1930*, p. 516); and Bill Jenks and Jerry Luna (*Early American Pattern Glass, 1850-1910* and *Identifying Pattern Glass Reproductions*).

Tom and Neila Bredehoft have done extensive research on George Duncan and Sons. In their opinion, there is no evidence to link any of these patterns to Duncan. The Bredehofts believe that a factory fire destroyed many of the Duncan molds in 1893.

Minnie Watson Kamm (*A First Two Hundred Pattern Glass Book*, p. 131) pictures an 1896 Co-Operative Flint advertisement from *China, Glass and Lamps* for Imperial, the pattern we know as Moon and Star Variant. In a footnote (p. 125), she states that Co-Operative Flint acquired these molds from the Wilson Glass Company of Tarentum, Pennsylvania, when Wilson went out of business in 1890. It seems that Kamm belongs neither in the camp of those who think these patterns originated with Duncan nor with those who think they originated with Co-Operative Flint.

Kamm, Revi, Innes, Jenks, and Luna all claim that Phoenix received these molds from Co-Operative Flint in 1937 as part of a bankruptcy settlement (not in 1929 as stated by Belknap and Ferson). Phoenix produced milk

An early catalog page displays tableware in the Lace & Dewdrop pattern. *Top row:* Tall footed celery, creamer, sugar, cup and saucer set; *Bottom row:* 10" plate, 8" plate, covered butter, sherbet on bread and butter plate. Kemple items numbers are shown.

glass in these molds for a few years in what they called their "Early American Glass Line" (Jenks, Luna, and Reilly, p. 192). The following explanation appears in *Identifying Pattern Glass Reproductions* (p. 193):

"Called Lace Dew Drop by Phoenix, this line included complete sets in milk white with either pearl or caramel luster or blue or pink-stain finishes that were marked with only a paper label.

"By July 1943, Phoenix had discontinued all tableware production and either scrapped or sold these and other molds. A letter dated December 14, 1943, from A.H. Brown of the Phoenix Glass Company to J. Stanley Brothers reported: 'We. . .are sorry to advise that this (Early American Line) has been withdrawn for the duration. The last stock we had of this was closed out to the Czecho-Slovak Glass Products Company of 45 West 34th Street, New York City.' At this time, H.M. Tuska of New York City (a distributor of glassware) acquired the molds to all four patterns from the Phoenix Glass Company."

LACE & DEWDROP

Lace & Dewdrop was one of the most important of the four patterns. From the 26 molds acquired, the Kemples made about 38 items. This was accomplished by reworking certain pieces as they came out of the mold. Lace & Dewdrop was made extensively in milk glass, with a few items in blue milk glass. Later, at the plant in Kenova, some items were produced in colored crystal. This pattern is well illustrated on pages 21-24, 51, 52, and 72.

Lace & Dewdrop consists of scallops; triangular, beaded sawteeth; beaded flower petals that alternate with larger beaded ovals; and a beaded horizontal band running around the middle. Even the underside of pedestaled bases (e.g. on the goblet) have this pattern. Since these molds

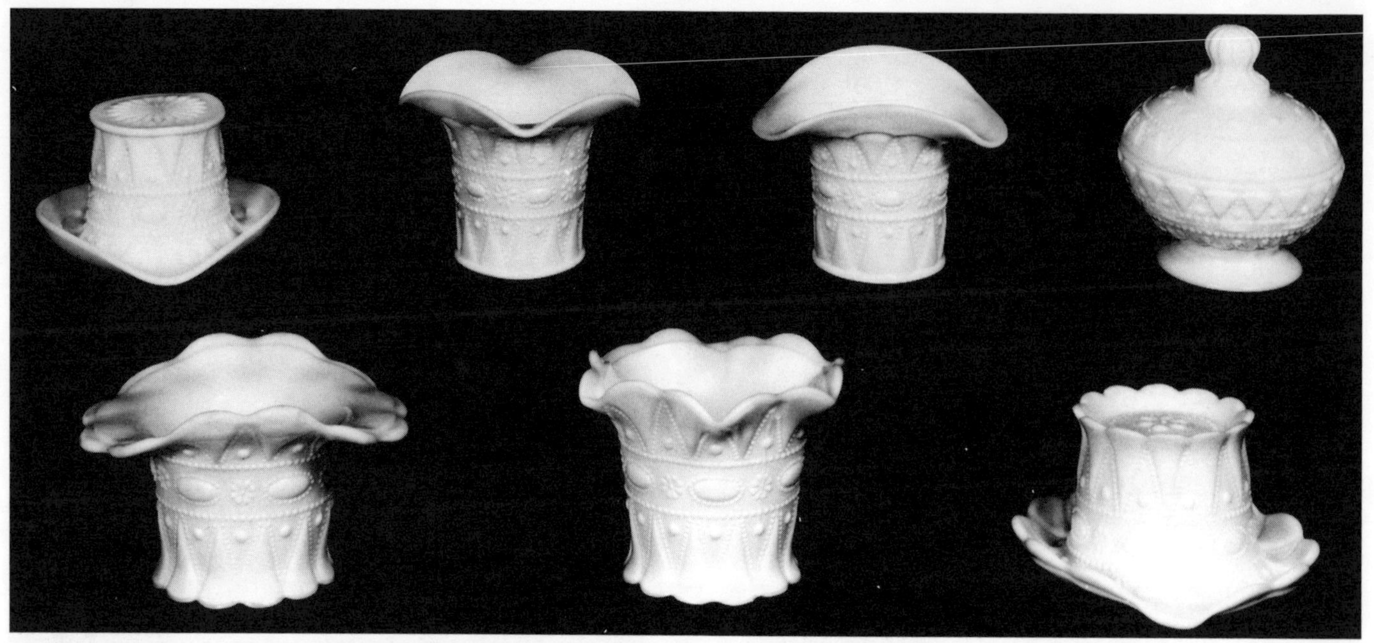

Variations on an original mold. *Top row:* No. 429 small hat, No. 425 small crimp vase, No. 426 small basket vase, No. 413 covered peanut jar; *Bottom row:* No. 410 large basket vase, No. 418 large crimp vase, and No. 430 large hat.

Kemple's tumbler and goblet set in Lace & Dewdrop, shown with 36 oz. water pitcher.
Kemple No. 407 tumbler, No. 409 pitcher, and No. 408 goblet.

were worn from use, pattern detail on Kemple items is less well-defined than on earlier Co-Operative or Phoenix pieces. Still, these Kemple reproductions have enough detail to be pleasing to the eye.

Kemple assigned line numbers in the 400 range to the Lace & Dewdrop wares. Items included the following: tall covered sugar and creamer; low open sugar and creamer; covered butter; spooner; 8" and 10" plates; 6", 8" and 10" bowls; 8" covered bowl; 4" sauce; tumbler; 8 oz. goblet; 36 oz. water pitcher; 4" basket vase; covered nut dish (with finial); sherbet; covered butter (flat finial); 6" and 8" compotes—covered and open; tall footed celery; 4$\frac{1}{2}$" candlesticks; cup and saucer; small and large crimped vases; small and large basket vases; small and large hats; 6" large candlestick; 10" footed cake plate; 8" footed float bowl; 6" handled basket; and a footed, handled basket.

Item numbers for these pieces are included in the photo captions. For those interested in specific item numbers, refer to the "400" listings in the Product Number Index, p. 146.

IVY-IN-SNOW

Another important acquisition from Tuska consisted of 25 molds in the Ivy-in-Snow pattern. From these molds Kemple produced about 44 different items. Line numbers for these wares fell in the 100s, but other patterns were also in this range. In fact, Kemple gave several Ivy-in-Snow pieces the same product numbers as items in the Yutec pattern, later made from McKee molds. Ivy-in-Snow items are illustrated on pages 25-27, and 53.

The Ivy-in-Snow pattern features sharp-edged ivy leaves, buds, and vines—all in relief. The background is finely stippled to create the snow effect. This pattern probably originated at Co-Operative Flint in the mid-1890s, where it was made in clear glass, sometimes with ruby-stain decoration. When the molds were acquired by Phoenix in 1937, this firm produced the four-piece table set in milk glass. These wares were marked only by paper labels.

At Kemple, Ivy-in-Snow was first produced in milk glass, then a few items were made in blue milk glass. In addition to paper labels, a "K" was added to some of the molds. The milk glass pieces were occasionally hand decorated. At the Kenova plant in the 1960s, some colored glass was also made in this pattern. Again, because of mold wear, Kemple's Ivy-in-Snow lacks the sharp lines and high relief of earlier production.

This extensive line included the following: 7", 8" and 9" oblong bowls; 4", 6" and 8" round bowls; 5" footed sherbet; 6" covered bowl; 5" and 7" covered candies; 6$\frac{1}{2}$" and 10" plates; footed cake plate; 8" oval banana split; 5" sauce; 3" cup; saucer; covered sugar; creamer; spooner; covered butter; tall celery; flare vase; cup-top and flute-top vases;

10" covered compote in the Ivy-in-Snow pattern, Kemple No. 135.

Kemple No. 124 36 oz. water pitcher in Ivy-in-Snow. The ivy leaves rest on a textured base, creating a "snowy" effect. (Photo by Harold E. Johnson, *Milk Glass*, 1959)

A catalog page of milk glass items in the Ivy-in-Snow pattern. A Moon & Star Variant bowl, as well as Sawtooth candlesticks have been included.

Ivy-in-Snow No. 116 creamer, No. 110 6½" plate, No. 115 covered sugar, No. 106 footed 5" sherbet, and No. 112 oval 8" banana split.

No. 141 Ivy-in-Snow flared vase, and No. 142 footed covered candy. Two variations on the same mold.

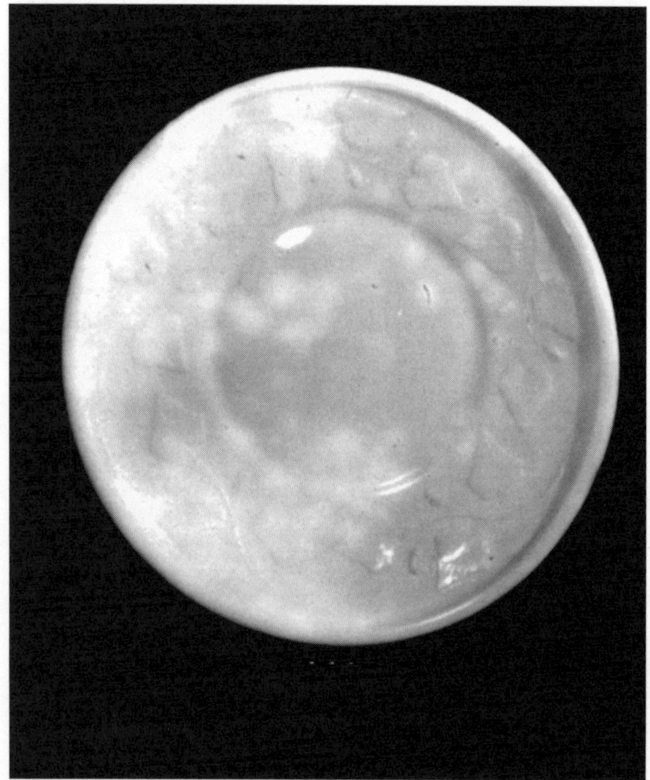

No. 111 10" plate in the Ivy-in-Snow pattern.

Ivy-in-Snow No. 127 Tall celery with crimped top, and No. 117 Tall celery with flared top.

An early Kemple Ivy-in-Snow catalog page. *Top row:* creamer, covered sugar, 6" covered bowl, covered butter, 7" covered candy; *Second row:* 10" plate, 8" oval banana split, boullion cup and saucer, covered compotes; *Third row:* 5" saucer with 3" cup, 5" footed sherbet, heart-shaped nappy, tumbler, 8 oz. goblet, candlesticks; *Bottom row:* crimp and flare celery, swing vases, flare vase, footed covered candy. Kemple item numbers are shown.

6-way and 4-way crimped vases; flared and crimped vase; swung vases; boullion cup; tumbler; tall mug; 8 oz. goblet; 3 and 5 oz. wines; top hat; candlestick; 7" bowl; heart nappy; 8" and 10" covered compotes; and 36 oz. water pitcher.

MOON AND STAR VARIANT

As the name implies, this pattern—also known as Jeweled Moon and Star—is inspired by an earlier pattern. The original Moon and Star features stars (or rosettes) in circles and tall, oval-shaped moons. In contrast, Moon and Star Variant has horizontally shaped ovals that connect around the ware. A row of undecorated ovals alternates with a row of ovals containing a star or rosette. The stem on footed pieces features a large "pineapple" or diamond-point knob.

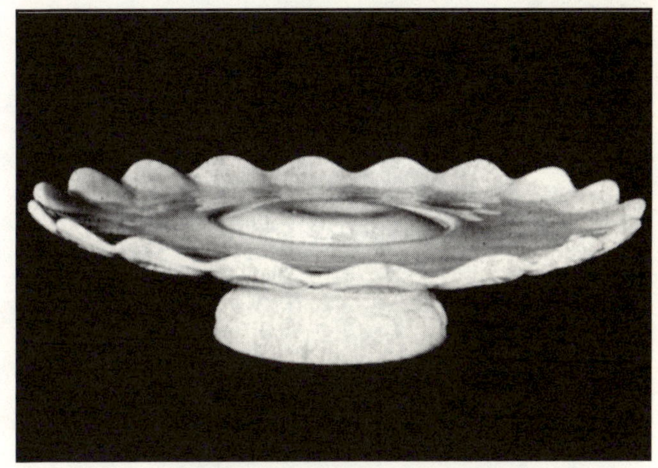

Footed 11" cake plate in the Moon & Star Variant pattern — Kemple No. 309

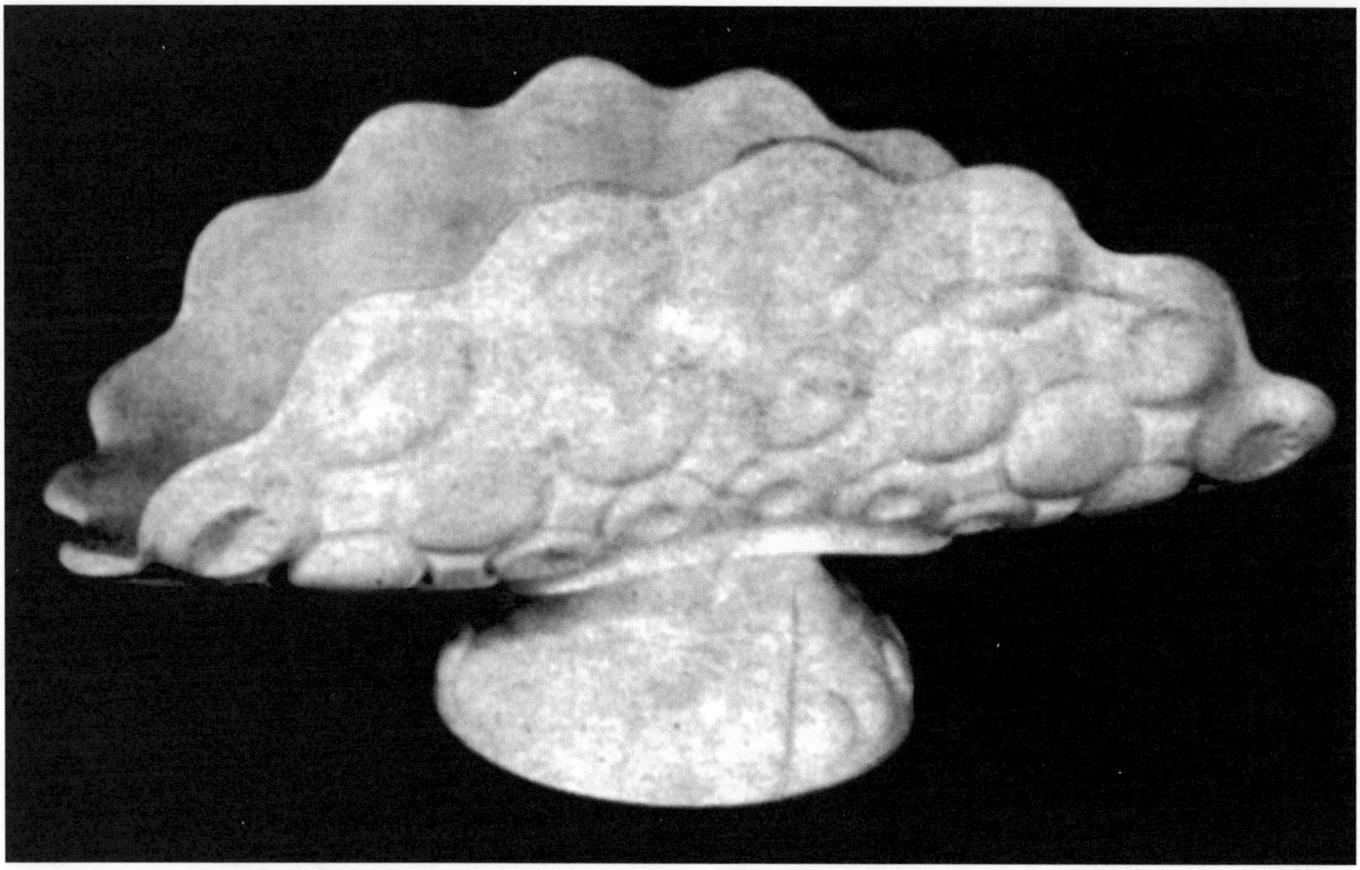

Footed banana boat in the Moon & Star Variant pattern, yet another variation
on the basic bowl mold — Kemple No. 308.

Moon & Star Variant footed compote with candlesticks — Kemple No. 304 and No. 307.

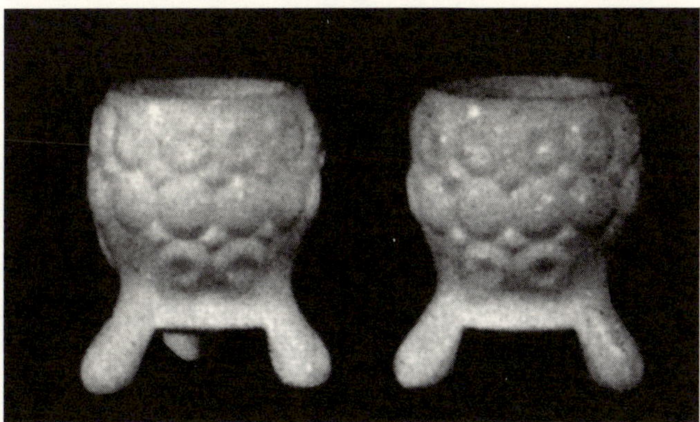

No. 312 3-footed candlestick holders in the
Moon & Star Variant pattern.

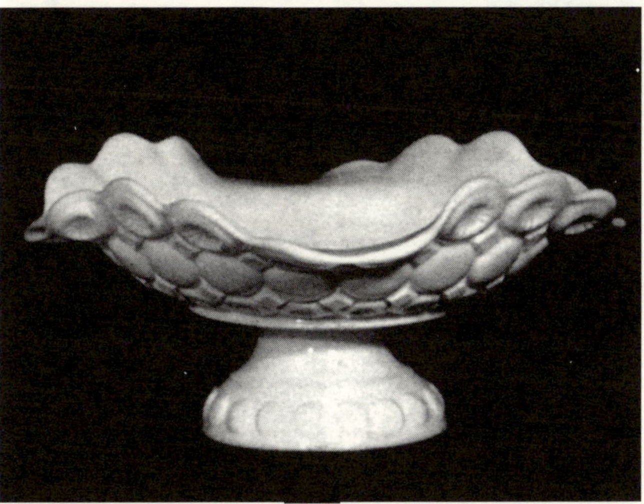

No. 311 11" footed crimp bowl, an example of how Kemple
could create several variations on one mold by crimping or
reshaping the edges.

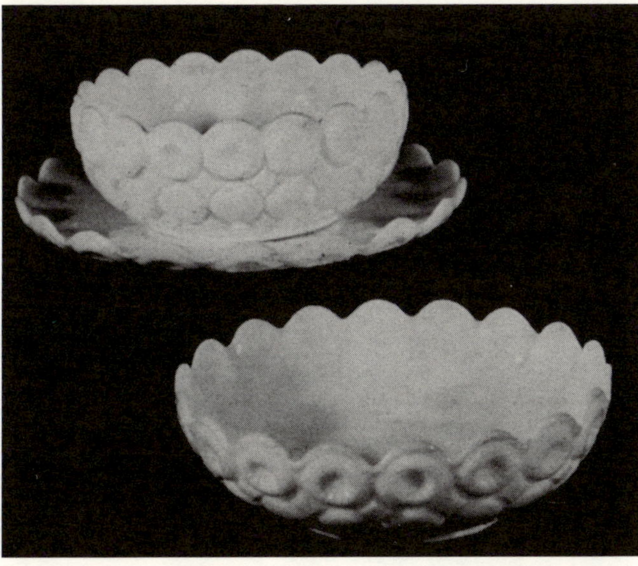

Moon & Star Variant No. 300 8" bowl resting in No. 302
11" flute bowl, pictured with the No. 301 10" bowl.

The Kemples purchased seven molds in this pattern from which they manufactured about 16 products with line numbers from 300-315. Our records list the following wares: 8" and 10" bowls; 12" cake plate; 11" flute bowl; 12" low banana boat; candlesticks; 11" crimped bowl; console set (bowl and candlesticks); footed compote; footed banana boat; 11" footed cake stand; 10" footed bowl; 11" footed crimped bowl; three-footed candlesticks; 10" handled basket; and a footed compote. As with the other patterns, these items were made in milk glass, blue, amber, and possibly other colors. In addition to the illustrations on pages 27-29, see pages 54, 69, and 79 in the color section for Moon & Star Variant.

BLACKBERRY

Blackberry may cause confusion because a similar pattern with this name was made by Hobbs Brockunier of Wheeling, West Virginia. Hobbs' Blackberry was later reproduced by Westmoreland in new molds.

Kemple's Blackberry, also called Dewberry, differs from the Hobbs' pattern in several respects. Whereas Hobbs' Blackberry has large, rounded, well-defined berries and large leaves, Co-Operative Flint's Dewberry (Kemple's Blackberry) has berries that are more triangular or spade-shaped. Also, the vines are more prominent in Kemple's Blackberry than in Hobb's.

Kemple acquired 14 molds in this pattern from which they made about 16 items. Having product numbers from

No. 203 36 oz. water pitcher in the Blackberry pattern.
The berries in Kemple's molds were pointed, not oval or
round as in the earlier Hobbs' Blackberry.
(Photo by Harold E. Johnson, *Milk Glass*, 1959)

Part of the Blackberry table setting — Kemple No. 204 goblet, No. 206 covered sugar, and No. 205 creamer.

Blackberry pattern 9" bowl, Kemple No. 208.

200-220, these include: 5" and 7" compote; 8" covered compote; 36 oz. pitcher; 8 oz. goblet; creamer; covered sugar; 4", 5", 6", 7", 8", and 9" bowls; wine; and 5" stemmed compote (sherbet). A few of these pieces had the berries and leaves decorated. All were made in milk glass. Later, the goblet was produced in amber and blue. The Blackberry pattern is pictured on pages 29-30, and 55.

MISCELLANEOUS TUSKA PURCHASES

In addition to the four patterns discussed above, the Kemples also bought molds from Tuska for three miscellaneous pieces. One item is the No. 76 *Hobnail* three-footed candlestick (p. 132). A second piece is a 7" No. 207 *Cabbage Leaf* plate (p. 49). The last, and most significant of the three, is the No. 40 *Sawtooth* candlestick, which remained in the Kemple line for several years (pp. 79, 89, 95, 96, 104, 105). The page numbers in parentheses indicate where the pieces are illustrated.

CONCLUSION

Taken together, the molds obtained from H.M. Tuska played a major role in the growth of the Kemple Glass Works. Evidence of this fact is found in Kemple's 1948 price list. Of the 93 items listed, 79 were produced in molds acquired from Tuska. Many of these wares continued to be made throughout the company's 25-year history.

Although the Kemple Glass Works never became a large company, its growth was significant. According to the East Palestine *Daily Leader* (April 10, 1951), the business had $500,000 in annual sales—a significant sum, especially in 1951. Kemple was able to build upon this level of production over the coming years.

CHAPTER FOUR
NEW LIFE FOR McKEE MOLDS

The largest group of molds which the Kemples acquired had previously belonged to the McKee Glass Company. Samuel and James McKee established S. McKee & Company in 1834 in Pittsburgh to produce window glass and bottles. The name then evolved to J. & F. McKee in 1850, and later in the year to Bryce, McKee & Company when the McKee brothers joined with James and Robert Bryce to manufacture flint glass.

By 1854, the connections had been severed and the Bryce brothers and McKee brothers went their separate paths. A third brother, Stewart McKee, joined in 1865.

After 1888, the company moved to Westmoreland County, Pennsylvania, settling in a town which was built to house the plant's workers. The town was named Jeannette (after Mrs. McKee), and was founded by H. Sellers McKee, then owner of the McKee plant.

In 1899, McKee & Brothers joined with other glass companies to form the National Glass Company. In 1903, however, the National was in serious financial trouble. The plant at Jeannette withdrew and reorganized as the McKee Glass Company. One of the largest glass factories under one roof in the United States, this firm was known as the McKee-Jeannette Glass Works from 1904-1910.

About 300 original McKee hand-pressed molds were sold to the Kemples from 1950-1957. A photo of the Kemple display at an early trade show in Pittsburgh (c. 1950) shows a few of the McKee covered animal dishes, such as the Duck, Horse, Dog, and Hen. Also, a Kemple advertisement in the April 1950 edition of *Crockery and Glass Journal* pictures the $5^{1}/_{2}$" Crouching Rabbit, Turkey, and Duck, on the split rib base.

Many of the McKee molds were scarce because during World War II, cast-iron molds were sold by the ton as scrap metal to the United States Government. What was left of the old McKee molds was stored in an underground tunnel beneath the original factory site. John and Geraldine Kemple spent three days in the storage cave, making their selections. The unusual names and designs of the molds attracted them, such as Aztec, Toltec, Sextec and Martec.

The Kemples bought some molds prior to the sale of McKee to the Thatcher Glass Company in 1951. At this time, the McKee plant was changing over from hand to machine operation. The majority of the molds could not be used with machine methods. Thatcher Glass ended up selling its interest in the McKee firm to the Jeannette Glass Company, located just ten blocks from the original McKee plant. The entire operation was then moved to the old McKee plant.

From 1956-57, the Kemples returned and purchased about 150 blown molds and five pressed molds for stoppers. Other stoppers were made off-hand by the skilled Kemple artisans. The October 1956 edition of *Crockery and Glass Journal* mentions 62 new molds acquired by the Kemples in that same year.

At no time did the Kemples wish to con the public into believing that their pieces were antique glass. To avoid any misunderstanding, they created a paper label stating "*Authentic Antique Reproductions* from an original mold," and giving the "Tec" name or pattern. As human errors did occur, a Kemple employee would occasionally put one "Tec" label on another "Tec" piece. Collectors should keep this in mind when examining the label on a piece of collectible glass.

According to Sandra McPhee Stout (*The Complete Book of McKee Glass*, p. 24), the McKee logo in script appeared on molds for milk glass hens and roosters of the 1870 era. Other information points to a later date —

Roberta Jones Odem inspects a Hen covered dish in the packing department at Kemple Glass.

perhaps the early 1890s. The Prescut trademark came into use between 1904 and the early 1930s to designate this new line of heavy pressed ware.

When Kemple Glass began its reproductions, it did not mark all of the acquired McKee molds with a "K," resulting in an occasional hard-to-identify piece. Other glass factories did purchase some of the "Tec" and "Innovation Cut" molds from Thatcher, but their pieces were on a more limited production and should not normally be confused with Kemple products.

For example, when co-author John Burkholder spotted a 6" rose bowl in the Plytec pattern at the Fenton gift shop, he wondered about the origin of the mold. Frank Fenton, former chairman of the Fenton Art Glass Company, told us that his company had purchased all the remaining McKee molds from Thatcher. In some cases, McKee had more than one mold for a given shape. The Kemples may have acquired one, but other companies may have purchased an identical mold. This explains how a Fenton rose bowl (with the Fenton logo) can be nearly identical to the Plytec rose bowl made by Kemple Glass Works.

PRESCUT LINE

McKee & Brothers Glass Company was the sole proprietor of its Press Cut (Prescut) Glass line. As the name implies, the line was intended to imitate the more expensive cut glass popular at the turn of the century. Many glass companies of this period had similar pressed wares that imitated cut glass.

At this time, deeply cut and ornate patterns were growing in popularity. The *Aztec* pattern of 1894 was reintroduced as part of this new line in 1901, and in 1902 the *Toltec* pattern was introduced. Both patterns offered numerous pieces in table sets and dinnerware. Andrew J. Smith, then president of McKee-Jeannette Glass Works, did his best to promote the full line of Aztec products. Because these wares were expensive, he emphasized "quality over cost." The reader can see the Aztec pattern in much greater detail by referring to pages 64, 65 and 66.

TOLTEC

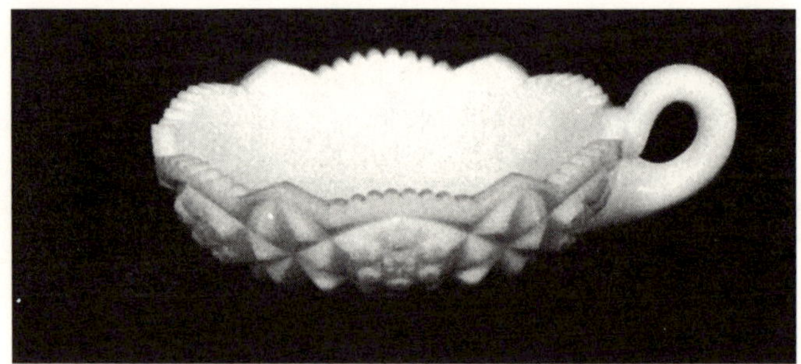

No. 216 Toltec 6" handled bon-bon in milk glass.

No. 215 Toltec tall creamer in milk glass.

AZTEC

Aztec—first of the Prescut patterns to be released by McKee glass—Kemple No. 195 9 oz. goblet

Kemple No. 203 Toltec 6" bowl and
No. 81 footed jelly, both in milk glass.
(Toltec is also illustrated on pages 56, 69, and 73.)

In 1906, the *Sextec* and *Martec* patterns came on the market in a full line of tableware. *Sunburst* was introduced in 1909 also as a complete table setting. The popularity of these patterns continued, and by 1915 the line was complete. The following illustrations of these patterns were taken from *The Complete Book of McKee Glass*, Stout, 1972.

McKee's "Tec" patterns were offered almost exclusively in clear, or crystal, glass. A pattern known as Rock Crystal (which Kemple did not purchase) was offered in Amber, Crystal, Green, and Rose-Pink.

McKee had 22 specifically named patterns—as well as some miscellaneous patterns—under the Prescut line, but to our knowledge, Kemple only purchased and pressed the *Aztec, Bontec, Carltec, Martec, Plutec, Plytec, Quintec, Rotec, Sextec, Toltec, Valtec, Wiltec, Yutec,* and *Sunburst* patterns. Once the original McKee molds became worn, some of the detail was lost in Kemple's reproductions, producing slight variations on the original. Some of the illustrations shown in this chapter are steel engravings taken from old McKee catalogs. These engravings (below) show the patterns more clearly than some of the milk glass pictures from Kemple brochures.

SEXTEC

Footed jelly in Sextec ("Flower & Garland") pattern, Kemple No. 69.

(Please refer to pages 69 and 71 to view more examples of this pattern.)

MARTEC

5" footed jelly bowl in Martec, Kemple No. 130.
(Martec is also illustrated on pages 68, 92, and 100.)

BONTEC

Kemple No. 75 Bontec 5" handled nappy.
(See page 67 for more items in the Bontec pattern.)

CARLTEC

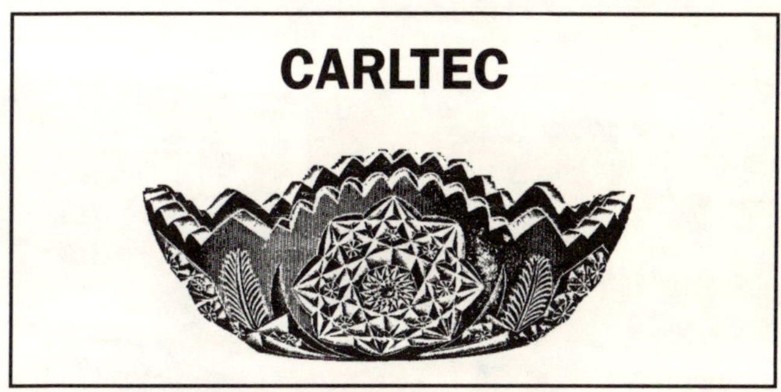

Kemple No. 83 Carltec 7" oblong bowl.
(Additional examples of Carltec appear on pp. 68 and 93.)

Wine bottle in the Plutec pattern, Kemple No. 524. (Plutec is also illustrated on page 59.)

PLUTEC

PLYTEC

QUINTEC

6¹/₂" bowl in Plytec, Kemple No. 74.
(Plytec is also illustrated on pages 63, 78, and 90.)

ROTEC

No. 167 Rotec creamer, also shown
in color on page 69.

Footed vase in Quintec, Kemple No. 66.
(Quintec is also illustrated on page 73.)

SUNBURST

Left to right: The Sunburst pattern in milk glass — Kemple item No. 663 ewer with spout,
No. 664 ewer with stopper, No. 662 bottle with stopper, No. 660 vase, No. 661 ewer with slant neck.

VALTEC

Valtec footed compote, Kemple No. 197.
(Valtec is also illustrated on page 69.)

WILTEC

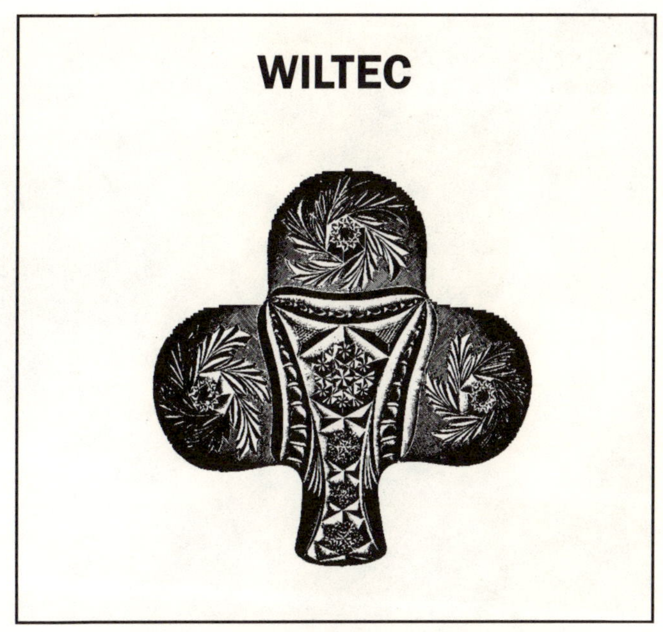

Kemple No. 103 Shamrock olive tray in Wiltec.
(Wiltec is also illustrated on page 69.)

YUTEC

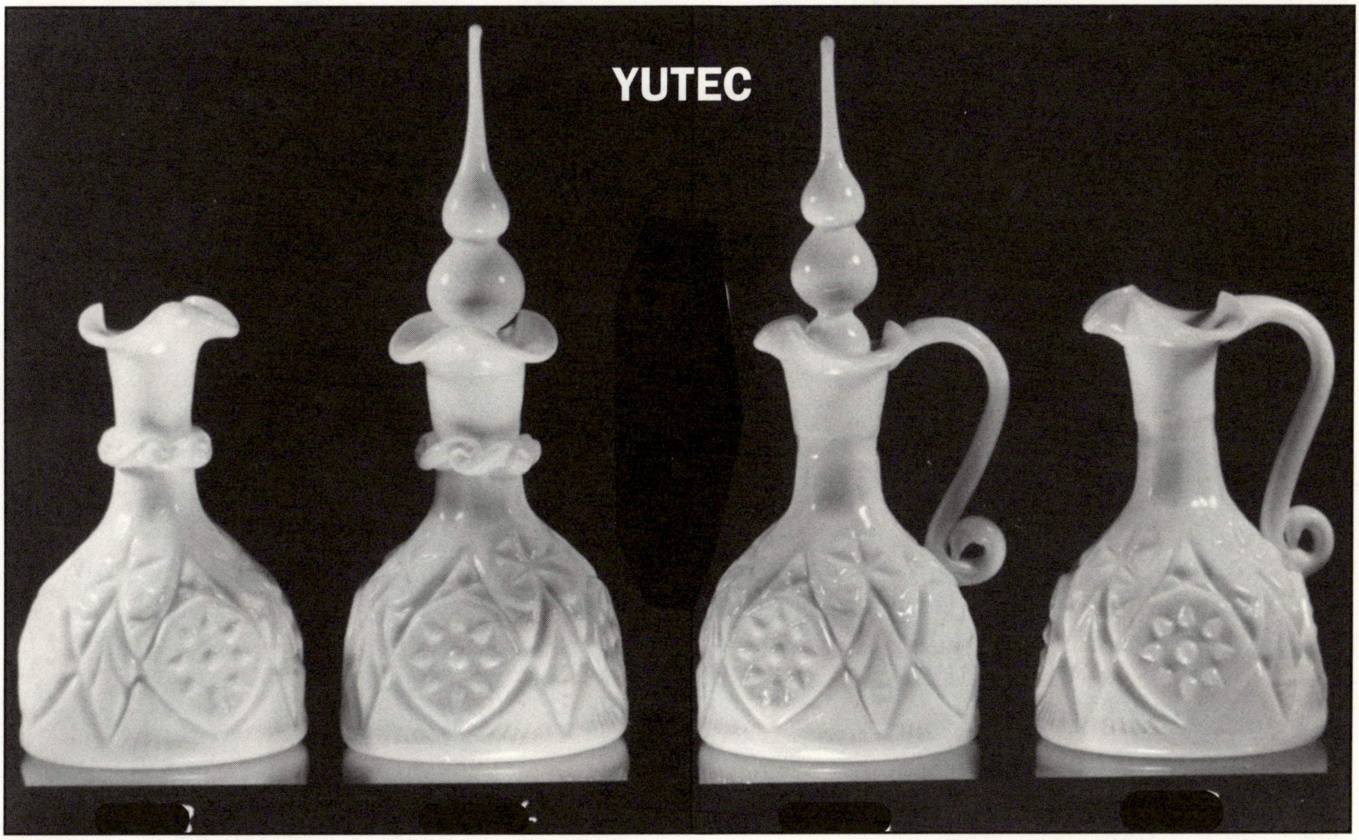

A picturesque assortment of the Yutec pattern in milk glass. *Left to right:* Kemple No. 653 decanter with rigaree and spout, No. 654 decanter with rigaree and stopper, No. 626 ewer with stopper, No. 625 ewer with ruffled spout and handle.

YUTEC

Kemple item No. 149, 8-piece Bride Set in the Yutec pattern, milk glass; consisting of sugar with cover, salt, pepper, tray, toothpick, and creamer with cover. This pattern features eight-pointed stars cut in relief.

The *Yutec* pattern, because of its popularity as a Kemple line, is pictured in many places throughout this book. The reader may refer to pages 56-59, and 70 for additional illustrations. One example of a popular Yutec item in the Prescut line is the No. 149 bride set (illustrated above), consisting of salt and pepper, covered sugar, covered creamer, toothpick holder, and tray. Another popular item was the No. 112 14-piece punch set, consisting of punch bowl, foot, and 12 cups (p. 58).

Kemple reproduced the "Tec" patterns in milk glass and, after 1960, colored glass, making them distinct from the McKee originals. An exhaustive list of Kemple's colors appears at the end of this chapter. However, some of the "Tec" patterns appeared in amber, amberina, amethyst, blue, cobalt blue, dark green, green, and the 1963 West Virginia Centennial Red. The popular Yutec bride set was available in milk glass, amber and dark green, and the *Sunburst* pattern (p. 34) was made mostly in milk glass. Some pieces had unusual color effects, such as No. 197, a frosted amber *Valtec* compote; No. 208, a *Toltec* toothpick in amberina; No. 72-2, the *Plytec* 7" rose bowl in 1963 Pink Slag; and No. 83, the *Carltec* 7" oblong bowl, also in 1963 Pink Slag.

INNOVATION CUT LINE

In 1917, the first of the Innovation Cut Glass lines (McKee No.410) was patented. The majority of these design patents were issued to Maurice A. Smith, who was at the time vice-president of McKee Glass.

Nut bowl in Innovation Cut, "V-Cane and Daisy." Kemple No. 129.

An ice tub in Innovation Cut, "Cane Panel and Daisy." Kemple item No. 148, formerly called McKee No. 410.

While McKee listed the varying designs by pattern number, collectors have coined descriptive names for many of these patterns, such as McKee No. 410, called "*Cane Panel & Daisy*" or "*V-Cane & Daisy*" (illustrated above), and McKee No. 414, "*Cane Band & Rose*". McKee's No. 414, the 14½" orange bowl with comport foot that we know as *Napoleon's Hat*, pictured below, was one of Kemple's more popular reproductions in this line.

Other pattern descriptions included "*Cane Panel*," "*Medallion & Diamond*," "*Sparkle*," "*Prince*," and "*Blazier*." McKee also produced a mold for "*Innovation Crackled*" glassware, which we know today as Kemple's *Natural Crackle*.

Kemple acquired only a portion of McKee's Innovation Cut line patterns for bowls, compotes, trays, ice tubs, cups, tumblers and jugs. No permanent trademark was applied to the Innovation molds, and once purchased by Kemple, they were sold according to new item numbers. However, identification is made easier by the fact that McKee produced the Innovation lines in mostly clear glass, whereas Kemple reproduced these lines in milk glass and the various colors listed at the end of this chapter.

Two-piece ensemble in the "Cane Band & Rose" pattern. Kemple item No. 89 on No. 93 6" compote foot. Also shown on page 76.

CANE BAND & ROSE

Kemple's popular "Napoleon's Hat" on base. This is Kemple No. 86, an Innovation cut piece in the "Cane Band and Rose" pattern. Several variations were made on this item, which serves as a banana boat or centerpiece for floral arrangements. A No. 141 Jubilee vase is pictured inside the bowl.

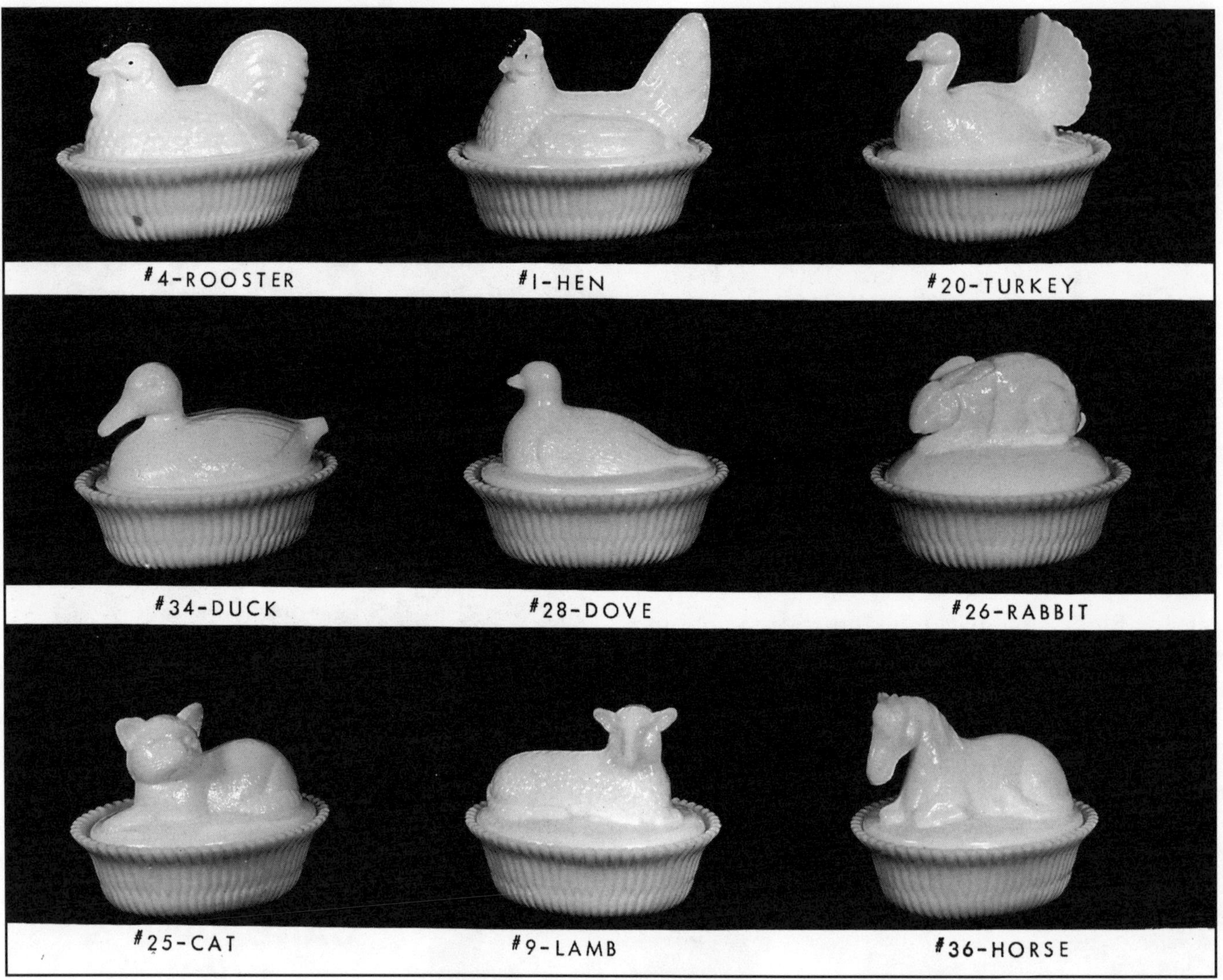

Catalog page showing Kemple's 5¹/₂" covered animal dishes with split-rib base. Pieces displayed are in milk glass, the Rooster and the Hen with red painted crowns. Kemple item numbers and names are shown.

COVERED ANIMAL DISHES

According to an advertisement in the April 1950 edition of *Crockery and Glass Journal*, Kemple was making reproductions of the McKee covered animal dishes in milk glass. These included a *Horse, Lamb, Turkey, Dog, Cat, Crouching Rabbit,* small *Hen on Nest,* and small *Rooster.* Renditions of a *Dove, Duck, Fox, Cow,* and *Lion* were most probably Kemple's later acquisitions. McKee's Hen and Rooster had been made in milk glass as early as the 1870s.

These covered animal dishes came in two sizes: the 5¹/₂" (small) size with a split-rib base, which included the Rooster, Hen, Turkey, Duck, Dove, Rabbit, Cat, Lamb, and Horse; and the 7¹/₂" (large) size with a basketweave base, which included the Cow, Lion, larger Rooster, larger Hen, and Fox.

Most of the 7¹/₂" basketweave covered animal dishes had the "K" trademark. The 5¹/₂" split-rib covered animal dishes were never marked. However, they do have two distinct characteristics which set them apart from similar dishes made by other companies: stippling under the rim of the lid, and rays on the bottom of the dish. On Kemple's dishes, the rays do not come together, but rather form a flat smooth spot in the center. A similar rabbit and a hen with a deeply scalloped tail were also made by Greentown.

Kemple produced covered animal dishes in milk glass, blue milk glass, amethyst, blue, celestial green, "End of Day," and honey amber. In addition, some of the 5¹/₂" dishes were made in amber, Centennial Red, cobalt blue and light blue. Kemple mixed colors within a piece, such as the small Hen on Nest which was blue with a white head and nest; the small Hen on Nest in amber with a white head and nest; and the small Rooster on Nest which was blue milk glass with a white head. Many of these colors were in production for only a short time.

Kemple's covered animal dishes, 7$^1/_2$" with basketweave base. Pieces displayed are in milk glass, the Rooster and the Hen with red painted crowns: Kemple No. 15 Fox; No. 24 Rooster; No. 31 Hen; No. 33 Cow; and No. 35 Lion. (Additional examples of covered animal dishes are illustrated on pages 83, 84, 100, and 102.)

MISCELLANEOUS WARE

In addition to the Prescut patterns, covered animal dishes, and Innovation Cut items, Kemple bought McKee molds for other tableware patterns. These included cruets, salts and peppers, caster sets, candlesticks, coasters, and ash trays. Rather than present this information chronologically, we have introduced each of the miscellaneous tableware patterns alphabetically for greater ease in reading.

The *Lacey Heart* molds that Kemple acquired made decorative bottles, cruets, decanters, and vases. This pattern was reproduced in milk glass, amber, blue and green. Cruets, decanters and a vase are shown on page 40.

By 1930, Prescut and other decorative wares were becoming outdated, and plainer, simpler designs were more fashionable. This accounts for the popularity of other McKee tableware patterns such as *Natural Crackle*, *Optic*, *Optic Swirl*, and *Swirl*. McKee introduced the Optic line in 1910, and produced it well into the 1930s. Kemple reproduced Optic and Optic Swirl in milk glass, amber and green; and Natural Crackle in colored glass vases, pitchers, and cruets. An unnumbered Optic Swirl pitcher was found in a Kemple collection in cranberry. These patterns are illustrated on pages 39-41.

Panel, *Panel Variant*, and *Rainbow* also became popular by 1930 because of the simplicity of their design.

Optic Swirl slender pitcher in colored glass, Kemple No. 624.

LACEY HEART

Lacey Heart ewers, decanters, and vase in milk glass.
Top row: Kemple No. 516 ewer with crimped spout, No. 519 bottle with stopper;
Bottom row: No. 518 ewer with tipped spout, No. 520 decanter with stopper and rigaree, No. 515 vase with rigaree.

(More Lacey Heart pieces are illustrated on page 59.)

NATURAL CRACKLE

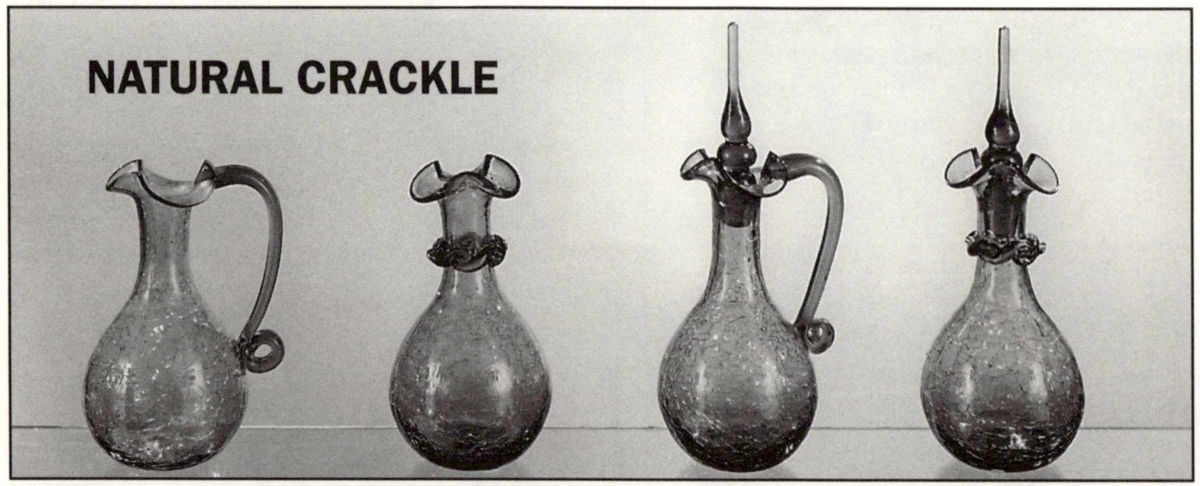

Natural Crackle pattern in colored glass: No. 548 ewer with ruffled spout, No. 549 vase with ruffled mouth and rigaree, No. 550 decanter with stopper and handle, and No. 638 decanter with rigaree.
No. 638 is also listed as No. 551 in some Kemple catalogs.

OPTIC

A catalog page displaying colored glassware in the Optic pattern. *Top:* bulbous vase with rigaree, bulbous vase with snake, ewer with elongated spout in green glass; *Bottom:* bulbous pitcher, vase with rigaree, pitcher. Kemple item numbers are shown. (Additional examples of Optic pieces are shown on pages 85 and 86.)

PANEL

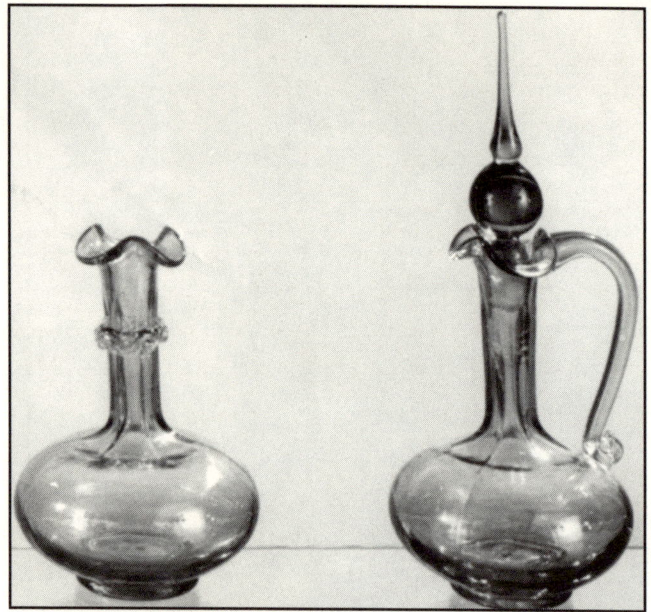

No. 612 Panel vase with rigaree; No. 614 Panel decanter with stopper and handle.

Ewer with handle and ruffled spout in the Panel pattern in colored glass, Kemple No. 613.

Rainbow was actually an earlier McKee pattern (1894) that was reissued with the other pressed lines after 1900. Panel and Panel Variant patterns appeared in various colored glass vases, pitchers, and cruets; Rainbow appeared in similar items, in milk glass, amber and green. Kemple also reproduced the *Rib Base* pattern in milk glass bottles, cruets, decanters, and vases. These patterns are illustrated on page 43.

The 1894 *Tappan*, commonly called "McKee's Pillow," was renamed "*Waffle & Button*" by Kemple. McKee produced the four-piece pattern in crystal glass (or crystal with ruby or amber stain), and sometimes in blue glass. The molds Kemple acquired were for toy glass spooners, creamers, covered sugars, and covered butters. Kemple reproduced Waffle & Button in milk glass, amber, amethyst, blue, Centennial Red, and green.

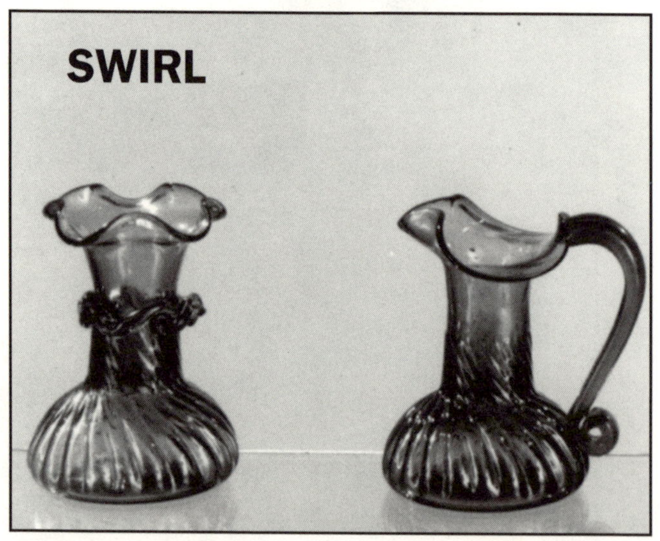

SWIRL

Kemple No. 605 Swirl vase with ruffled mouth and rigaree; No. 606 Swirl ewer with handle.

From *The Complete Book of McKee Glass*, Stout, 1972 — metal engraving of "McKee's Pillow," renamed "Waffle and Button" by Kemple: No. 175 miniature sugar with cover, No. 174 miniature spooner, No. 176 miniature creamer, and No. 177 miniature butter with cover.

This photograph demonstrates how the hand-finishing process at Kemple Glass could produce several different pieces from one mold. The Kemple pieces above (Nos. 510 - 514) have the same Rainbow base. Yet by adding a stopper to the No. 511 vase with rigaree, it becomes the No. 513 decanter or bottle. By adding a handle or crimped spout to the No. 511 vase with plain neck, it can be made into the No. 510 or No. 512 ewer.

Tableware in the Rib Base pattern in milk glass. *Top:* No. 507 ewer with elongated spout, No. 505 ewer with ruffled spout; *Bottom:* No. 508 decanter with stopper and handle, No. 506 vase with rigaree and ruffled top, and No. 509 bottle with rigaree and stopper.

Less extensive tableware patterns, of which the Kemples only made a few pieces, are also listed alphabetically and include *Banzantine, Champion, Hobstar & Fan, Pineapple, Sandwich, Sawtooth,* and *Sunburn.* Banzantine items were made in milk glass, amberina, dark green and green. The Sandwich pattern was made in milk glass, amberina and green. These patterns are illustrated on pages 44 and 45, with the exception of the Banzatine, for which no photographs were provided with Everett Miller's original draft.

According to Kyle Husfloen (*Collector's Guide to American Pressed Glass, 1825-1915,* 1992), Champion was another early McKee pattern (1894), reissued with the other pressed lines after 1900, and originally manufactured in clear, or clear with ruby or amber stain. Emerald green or other colors were extremely scarce. The Kemples made salt dips and condiment holders in this pattern, and reproduced the Hobstar & Fan compote in milk glass, amber, amethyst, blue and dark green.

McKee manufactured the Sawtooth (Diamond) pattern from 1859-1865, originally in clear or milk glass. Other colors for this line, such as amber, blues, or yellow were very rare. Kemple reproduced this pattern in candlesticks and water pitchers in a variety of colors.

Kemple No. 528 Champion vase with rigaree and ruffled mouth, No. 526 Champion cruet with stopper, and No. 529 Champion cruet with handle.

SAWTOOTH

Kemple No. 40 Sawtooth candlestick, also shown in color on page 79.

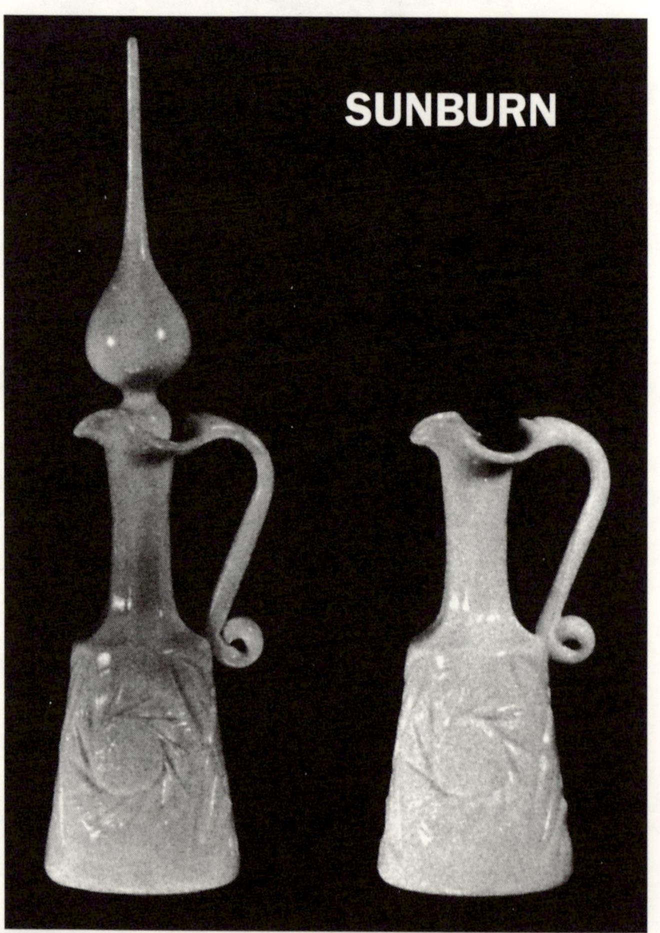

At first glance, the Sunburn pattern looks similar to McKee's Sunburst. However, the sun is larger in this design, and the base of these pieces is narrower. In milk glass, Kemple No. 652 decanter with stopper, and item No. 649 ewer. Both pieces were made from the same mold.

HOBSTAR & FAN

No. 49 Hobstar & Fan covered footed candy in milk glass with No. 45 matching covered butter.

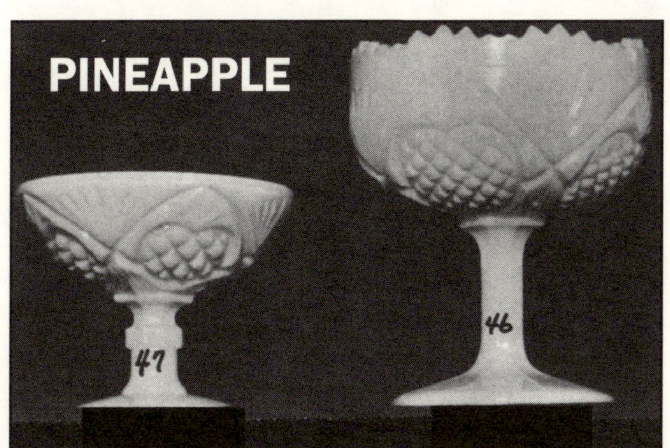

PINEAPPLE

Kemple item No. 47 low compote and No. 46 tall compote in Pineapple.

In addition to tableware patterns, the Kemples also purchased McKee molds for miscellaneous novelty items, consisting of only single pieces created in unique patterns. They are listed alphabetically, and include an *Art Dressed* vase, a *Cherub* toothpick holder, the *Eiffel Tower* candlestick, a matching *Gypsy Kettle* ash tray and toothpick, a hand-shaped ash tray appropriately described as the *Helping Hand*, the *Horse Shoe* pen rack, the *Lincoln Hat* toothpick, a *Westward Ho* goblet with Deer and Buffalo design, and a *Wooden Tub* salt. These miscellaneous items were reproduced by Kemple in a variety of colors, but the No. 101 Westward Ho goblet was found in a Kemple collection in an unusual vaseline and amethyst slag. They are illustrated on pp. 45-46.

SANDWICH

Kemple items No. 191 creamer and No. 189 mug, in the Sandwich pattern.

GYPSY KETTLE

Kemple item No. 242 and No. AM242, matching ash tray and toothpick in the Gypsy Kettle design.

Above: No. 200 Wooden Tub master salt;
Below: No. 283 Horseshoe pen rack.

WOODEN TUB

HORSESHOE

Three phases of pressed glass production: one worker gathers hot molten glass, another presses the mold, and a third boy stands by with an asbestos paddle, on which the fired glass piece will be carried to the annealing lehr.

COLORED GLASS PRODUCTION

This chapter on the McKee molds is a fitting place to discuss the introduction of colored glass to the manufacturing lines. Stout writes that "McKee had been ahead of its time in colored glassware" (Stout, p. 22). Early on, McKee Glass Company was a forerunner especially in the depression era colors: transparent ruby, pink, green, amber, and blue. By 1904, the company was manufacturing its most popular "Rose-Pink."

However, many of the molds which Kemple acquired were not originally produced in color by McKee Glass Company. Kemple Glass Works' contribution, in fact, was to reproduce these McKee lines in a wide variety of colors and blends.

In 1960, at the Kenova factory site, Kemple began producing colored glass, introducing a line of more than a dozen different colors that would eventually surpass its milk glass production. Not all of Kemple's reproductions were made in all colors, nor were all colors in production all the time, so we have provided an approximate chronology of their use:

1945-1970 — white milk glass
1951-1956 — blue milk glass
1958 — dark green
1960-1963 — amethyst (several shades)

1960-1961 — cobalt blue
1960-1966 — green
1960-1970 — blue (and teal)
1960-1970 — Golden Glow (honey amber)
1962-1964 — End of Day (slag)
1963-1970 — amberina
1963 — West Virginia Centennial Red
1964 — gray milk glass
1966 — light lemon/vaseline
1966 — smoke amber
1966 — amethyst opalescent

Kemple's color production was significant especially to the McKee mold purchases, because every color Kemple made was represented in these molds. Not every McKee piece was made in all colors, but we can definitively say that every color Kemple made was represented in at least one of the McKee reproductions.

CONCLUSION

Those antique molds that the Kemples acquired from an underground storage cave did enhance their lines of popular glassware, and proved to be an innovation not only for the original buyers, but also today's collectors. Most collectors would agree that the Kemples' decision to put the discontinued molds back into production was a good one. The McKee molds were used to make high quality glass at the turn of the century, and one could say that John and Geraldine Kemple and company gave "new life" to these old molds.

CHAPTER FIVE
KEMPLE GLASS IN COLOR

NOTES ON THE COLOR PAGES

Pages 49-94 feature photographs of approximately 800 pieces of Kemple glass, mostly from the collection of co-author John Burkholder, taken for the express purpose of illustrating this book. Items on a page are often grouped by *type of ware* (plates, covered animal dishes), *pattern* (Blackberry, Lace and Dewdrop), or *color* (Gray, End-of-Day); however, some pages have an assortment of miscellaneous pieces. Each photograph contains a headline which describes how the items have been grouped.

The pieces shown in each photograph are assigned figure numbers for identification throughout the book, which run from **1.** to **796.** The caption entries below each photograph often include the following information for the pieces shown: the Kemple item number, pattern name, and type of ware (e.g., figure **480.** No. 151 V-Cane & Daisy ice tea). Size dimensions and other physical descriptions appear directly in the captions for plates, covered animal dishes, and other pieces where the information has been made available to us. In some cases, item numbers (or other details) have been omitted, because this information is unavailable.

Certain practices are followed to best utilize space. For example, since page 49 shows only plates, the category "Plates" appears as a headline in the photograph, and "Plate" is not repeated for each individual entry. When two or more adjacent items have the same pattern, the name may appear only once.

For example, the first two entries read:

1-2. Sheaf of Wheat, No. 41 8" and No. 16A 6½".

This means that figure **1.** is a No. 41 Sheaf of Wheat 8" plate, and figure **2.** is a No. 16A Sheaf of Wheat 6½"

plate. "No. 41" and "No. 16A" are the item numbers that Kemple assigned to these pieces in company catalogs. The reader can use this item number to find out more detailed information about each piece, in the item number index which begins on p. 137.

Pages 95-112 reproduce pages from Kemple, Wheatonware, and Wheatoncraft catalogs. The figure numbers in the Kemple catalog pages are Kemple item numbers, sometimes preceded by letters which refer to the color of the item or line. Color code entries include: ED (End-of-Day), FR or GR (Amberina), B (Blue), G (Amber or Honey Amber), AM (Amethyst), and E (Celestial Green). Figure numbers in the Wheatonware and Wheatoncraft catalog pages are Wheaton item numbers, and *are not* included in the item number index on page 137.

Captions for this section are less detailed, but they do provide an overview of the wares shown. Although the catalog pages include many pieces that have already appeared in the color section (pages 49-94), these reprints also show items not previously illustrated, as well as later production from Kemple molds by Wheaton Industries.

Our publisher recommended that prices be placed in an index (Value Guide), rather than within the captions. This makes future revisions of the book less difficult.

The first section of this index prices figures **1.- 796.** (pages 49-94), according to their figure number. The following section prices the catalog page items by the item number included in the picture. Prices for identical items shown in both sections should be the same, but differences in color may account for some variations. The Value Guide begins on page 154.

PLATES

1 - 2. No. 41 and No. 16A Sheaf of Wheat 8" and 6½"
3 - 4. No. 204A and No. 204 Maple Leaf 6½" and 9"
5 - 6. No. 14 Sheaf of Wheat 7½" decorated and plain
7 - 8. No. 16A and No. 14 Sheaf of Wheat 6½", 7½"

9 - 12. No. 16 Panel Peg 7"—Monk, George Washington, Fruit, and Monk designs
13. No. 975 Open Edge 8"
14. No. 16 Panel Peg 7"
15. No. 207 Cabbage Leaf 7"

PLATES

<table>
<tr><td>16 - 18.</td><td>No. 38 Shell & Club 9½"</td><td>21.</td><td>No. 17 Lovers' Knot 8½"</td><td>25.</td><td>No. 16B Lacy Heart 7½"</td></tr>
<tr><td>19.</td><td>Unfinished Lovers' Knot</td><td>22 - 23.</td><td>No. 202 Inverted Heart 7"</td><td>26.</td><td>No. 29 Angel Head 8½"</td></tr>
<tr><td>20.</td><td>No. 30 Shell & Club 7"</td><td>24.</td><td>No. 30 Shell & Club 7"</td><td>27.</td><td>No. 17 Lovers' Knot 8½"</td></tr>
<tr><td></td><td></td><td></td><td></td><td>28.</td><td>No. 42 101-Open Edge 8½"</td></tr>
</table>

29. No. 419 footed celery	**36.** No. 414 covered butter	**42.** No. 420 candlestick 4^1/$_2$"
30. No. 405 covered bowl 8"	**37.** No. 400 tall covered sugar	**43.** No. 422 bowl 10"
31. No. 404 covered bowl 6"	**38.** No. 401 tall creamer	**44.** No. 420 candlestick 4^1/$_2$"
32. No. 415 compote 6"	**39 - 40.** No. 412 sherbet on the No. 423 saucer	**45.** No. 406 sauce 4"
33. No. 413 covered compote 8"	**41.** No. 431 candlestick 6"	**46.** No. 411 covered nut dish
34. No. 427 creamer		**47.** No. 51 covered peanut jar
35. No. 428 sugar		

48. No. 416 plate 10"	**53.** No. 410 crimped dish 4"	**60.** No. 410 large basket vase
49. No. 424 and 423, cup and saucer set	**54.** No. 410 basket vase 4"	**61.** No. 421 small crimped basket vase
50. No. 409 pitcher 36 oz.	**55.** No. 407 tumbler	**62.** No. 430 large hat
51. No. 408 goblet 8 oz.	**56.** No. 409 crimped pitcher 36 oz.	**63.** No. 410 large basket vase
52. No. 408 flared compote	**57.** No. 418 large crimped vase	
	58 - 59. No. 410 crimped vases	

64. No. 117/5 flared celery
65. No. 133 covered 8" compote
66. No. 117/3 crimped vase
67. No. 142 footed, covered candy
68. No. 124 water pitcher 36 oz.
69. No. 113 saucer, No. 114 cup
70. No. 110 plate 6½"
71. No. 111 plate 10"

72. No. 125 candlestick
73. No. 104 covered 8" bowl
74. No. 125 candlestick
75. No. 122 wine 5 oz.
76. No. 121 goblet 8 oz.
77. No. 120 tall mug
78. No. 119 tumbler

79. No. 52 footed, covered peanut
80. No. 115 covered sugar
81. No. 116 creamer
82. No. 114 cup 3"
83. No. 104 bowl 8"
84. No. 112 oval banana split 8"
85. No. 129 heart nappy

MOON & STAR VARIANT

86. No. 304 candlestick
87. No. 306 footed compote
88. No. 304 candlestick
89. No. 301-A cake plate 12"

90. No. 310 footed 10" cake
91. No. 312 3-footed candlestick
92. No. 301 bowl 10"
93. No. 312 3-footed candlestick

94. No. 308 footed banana boat
95. No. 304 stretched candle
96. No. 307 footed compote
97. No. 305 crimped 11" bowl
98. No. 303 low 12" banana boat

BLACKBERRY

99. large painted compote	**104.** No. 203 pitcher 36 oz.	**110 - 111.** No. 204 goblets
100. No. 220 footed 5" compote with lid	**105.** No. 206 sugar	**112.** No. 206 flared sugar
101. No. 206 sugar without cover	**106.** No. 205 creamer	**113 - 114.** tumblers
102. No. 209 bowl 8"	**107.** No. 220 5" compote	**115.** No. 212 bowl 5"
103. No. 205 creamer	**108.** Large compote	**116 - 117.** tumblers
	109. No. 206 covered sugar	

118. No. 97 V-Cane & Daisy
3½ pt. jug
119. No. 46 Pineapple tall jelly
120. No. 25 Lady's Boot vase
121. No. 97 Yutec chalice
122. No. 156 Cane Panel
3-toed round bowl
123. No. 64 Wedding Jar candy
124. No. 256 Southern Belle

125. No. 257 Colonial Lady
126. No. 258 Victorian Lady
127 - 128. No. 259B Dutch Girl and
No. 259A Dutch Boy bookends
129. Cat paperweight
130. No. 27 Helping Hand ash tray
131 - 132. No. 19A Mary and
No. 19B Jesus plaques
133. No. 15 Cabbage Rose mug

134. No. 215 Toltec tall creamer
135. Chain links
136 - 138. Waffle & Button No. 175
sugar, No. 176 creamer and
No. 177 covered butter
139. No. 288 Shell salt dip
140. No. 12 Indian Chief wall
match holder
141. No. 194 Rainbow wine

MILK GLASS ASSORTMENT

142. Sunburst whimsey vase
143. Splatter cruet
144. Yutec whimsey
145. No. 641 Optic cruet
146. No. 298 lamp base
147 - 148. Sunburst whimseys
149. No. 51 Lace & Dewdrop
nut dish, bottom

150. Innovation celery, unidentified
151. Innovation tray, unidentified
152. Prince 2-handled nappy
153. Yutec whimsey
154. Champion cup
155. Yutec whimsey
156. No. 52-I Plain 6" bowl with
Ivy design

157. Champion whimsey
158 - 160. Sunburst whimsey
pitchers
161. Yutec whimsey
162. Champion whimsey
163 - 164. No. 2 Yutec whimseys
165. No. 31 Hen on Nest 7$\frac{1}{2}$"
166. Pineapple bowl

YUTEC

167

168

169

170

171

172

173

174

175

167. No. 97 chalice
168. No. 121 round 4½" nappy
169. No. 149 bride set tray

170. No. 123 tumbler
171. No. 128 water pitcher
172. No. 139 crimped spooner

173. No. 106 oblong 10" bowl
174. No. 109 compote
175. No. 112 14 pc. punch set—
bowl, foot and 12 cups

CRUETS, DECANTERS, EWERS AND VASES

176. No. 522 Plutec vase
177. No. 518 Optic ewer with tipped spout
178. No. 515-N Lacey Heart vase with wide mouth
179. No. 516 Lacey Heart ewer
180. No. 656 Yutec ship decanter
181. No. 626 Yutec decanter with stopper

182. No. 534 Panel cruet
183. Panel vase whimsey
184. No. 502 Toltec pitcher
185. No. 500 Toltec vase
186 - 187. Toltec vase whimseys
188. No. 512 Rainbow ewer with tipped spout
189. No. 511 Rainbow decanter
190. Rainbow whimsey bowl

191. Sunburst pitcher
192. Sunburst cruet with stopper
193. No. 605 Swirl whimsey
194. No. 605 Swirl whimsey
195. No. 606 Swirl ewer with handle
196. No. 529 Champion ewer with crimped spout
197. No. 528 Champion vase with ruffled mouth

198 - 199. No. 199 Beaded Scroll 7" pin tray and No. 44 covered pin box

200. No. 10 Scroll Variant dresser tray 7$\frac{1}{2}$" x 10"

201. No. 8 Cabbage Rose round dresser box

202. No. 6 Heavy Scroll dresser tray

203. No. 6 Scroll with Flower small collar box

204. No. 4 Scroll 9" dresser tray

205 - 206. No. 39 Scroll Variant covered cigar jars

207. No. 2 Scroll with Flower rectangular dresser box

208. No. 43 Heart pin tray

209. painted pin tray

210 - 212. Beaded Scroll assorted pin trays

213. No. 155 Versailles dresser box, with the Kemple "K"

214. No. 12 Fleur de Lis powder box

215. No. 155 Versailles covered dresser box

216. No. 7 Scroll with Fleur de Lis round dresser box

217. No. 8 Cabbage Rose round dresser box

218. No. 18-V Scroll with Flower covered hankie box

219. Scroll No. 4 tray, No. 13 jewel box, and No. 12 powder box

220. No. 54 Cabbage Rose oval covered jewel box

221. No. 10 Scroll Variant dresser tray, with No. 147 Versailles cigarette box and No. 154 Versailles dresser box

NOVELTY ITEMS ASSORTMENT

222 - 226. No. 210 Coal Bucket with Bail ash trays
227 - 231. No. 245 Basket Weave toothpicks
232 - 237. No. 32 Puss-in-Boots pointed toe, solid
sole slippers
238 - 241. No. 5 Pansy Flower 3-handled toothpicks
242 - 247. No. 178 Indian Chief standing toothpick
holders
248 - 252. No. 209 Lincoln Hat toothpicks

253 - 260. No. 206 Pony & Cart toothpicks
and ash trays
261 - 262. No. 243 Gypsy Kettle toothpicks
263. No. 242 Gypsy Kettle ash tray
264 - 265. No. 243 Gypsy Kettle toothpicks
266 - 268. No. 201A novelty Wooden Tubs 3" x 2²/₃"
269 - 270. No. 201 Wooden Tub individual salts

NOVELTY ITEMS ASSORTMENT

271 - 289. Waffle & Button child's set No. 175 covered sugars, No. 174 spooners, No. 176 creamers, No. 177 covered butters
290 - 291. No. 162 Basket toothpicks
292. No. 73 miniature Toast mug
293 - 296. No. 21 Chick egg cups
297. No. 282 V-Cane & Daisy toothpick
298. No. 278 Scroll Variant hexagonal toothpick
299 - 300. No. 277 Scroll Variant square toothpicks
301. No. 221 Cherub (or Peek-a-boo) toothpick
302. No. 262 Indian ash tray
303. No. 47 Trunk treasure chest
304. No. 993 Mary & Child plate

305. No. 267 large Easter egg
306. No. 265 Hatchet figurine
307. No. 8 Cabbage Rose round dresser box
308. No. 43 Heart pin tray
309 - 310. whimsey toothpicks
311. No. 180 Flo paperweight
312 - 313. No. 636 Optic creamers
314. No. 635 Optic sugar
315. No. 180 Flo paperweight
316 - 318. No. 223 Ribbed 4-toe salt dips
319 - 321. miscellaneous marbles
322 - 323. No. 103 Yutec salts
324. unidentified oblong open salt

PLATES

325. Plytec 9^1/$_2$"
326. No. 38 Shell & Club 9^1/$_2$"
327. No. 29 Angel Head 8^1/$_2$"
328. No. 110 Ivy-in-Snow 6^1/$_2$"

329. No. 11 Lacy Heart 6"
330. No. 16A Sheaf of Wheat 6^1/$_2$"
331. Plytec 8^1/$_2$"
332. No. 204 Maple Leaf-Open Edge

333. No. 250 Sandwich 8"
334. No. 30 Shell & Club 7"
335. No. 16B Lacy Heart 7^1/$_2$"
336. No. 250 Sandwich 9^1/$_2$"

AZTEC

337. No. 62 footed 7" bon bon in blue
338. No. 62 footed 7" bon bon in amberina
339. No. 62 footed 7" bon bon in green
340. No. 62 footed 7" bon bon in vaseline
341. No. 62 footed 7" bon bon in cobalt
342. No. 62 footed 7" bon bon in amber
343. No. 62 footed 7" bon bon in milk glass

344. No. 62 footed 7" bon bon in green
345. No. 62 footed 7" bon bon in amethyst
346. No. 195 goblet 9 oz.
347. No. 197 cordial 1 oz. in amethyst
348. No. 197 cordial 1 oz. in amberina
349. No. 196 large 3 oz. wine

AZTEC

350 - 351. No. 181 cracker jars
352. No. 144 vase 10"
353. No. 62/2 fluted bon bon on stem
(a variation on No. 62 footed bon bon)
354. No. 96 handled 6" nappy
355. No. 145-C fluted 7" bon bon in amberina

356. No. 145-C fluted 7" bon bon in light blue
357. No. 145-C fluted 7" bon bon in amber
358. No. 78 covered butter
359. No. 85 spooner
360. No. 145 covered sugar or candy
361. No. 84 creamer

AZTEC

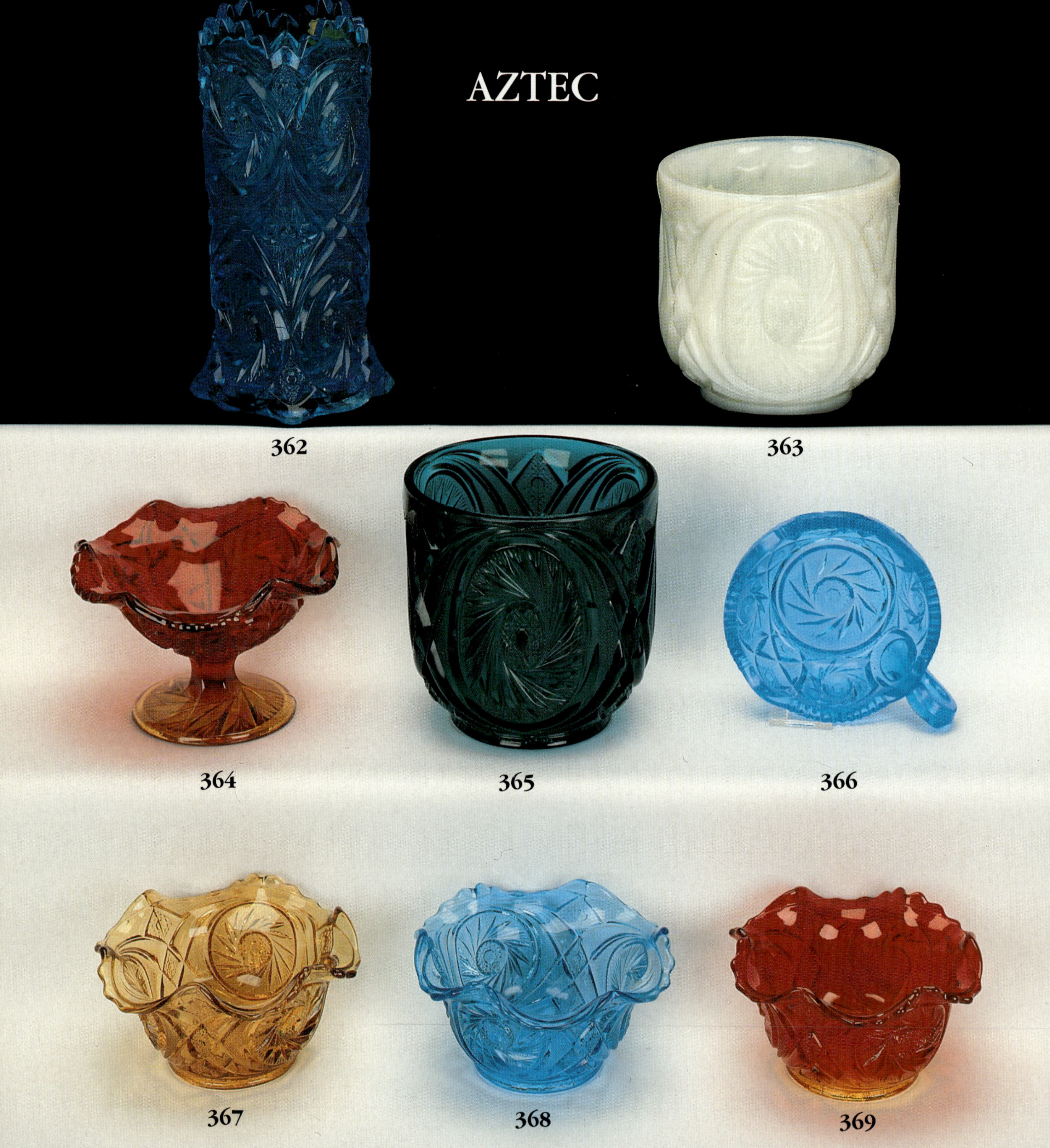

362. No. 144 vase 10"
363. No. 181 cracker jar
364. No. 62 footed bon bon
365. No. 181 cracker jar

366. No. 96 handled 6" nappy
367. No. 145-C fluted 7" bon bon in amber
368. No. 145-C fluted 7" bon bon in light blue
369. No. 145-C fluted 7" bon bon in amberina

BONTEC

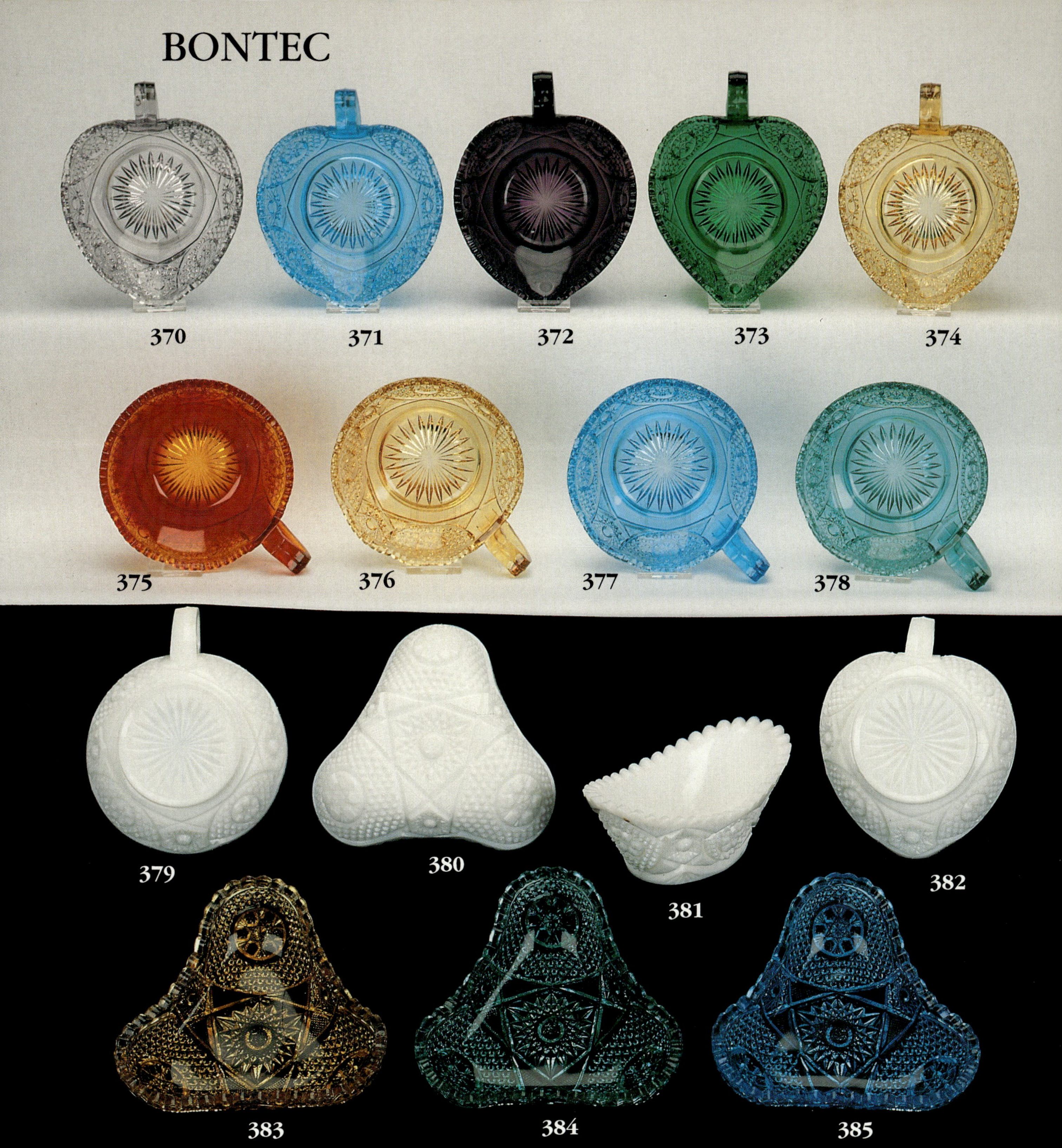

370. No. 99 Heart handled bon bon in light amethyst
371. No. 99 Heart handled bon bon in cobalt blue
372. No. 99 Heart handled bon bon in dark amethyst
373. No. 99 Heart handled bon bon in green
374. No. 99 Heart handled bon bon in amber
375. No. 75 handled 5" nappy in amberina
376. No. 75 handled 5" nappy in amber
377. No. 75 handled 5" nappy in cobalt blue

378. No. 75 handled 5" nappy in blue
379. No. 75 handled 5" nappy in milk glass
380. No. 82 triangular bon bon
381. No. 77-A Boat-shaped bon bon
382. No. 99 Heart handled bon bon in milk glass
383. No. 82 triangular bon bon in amber
384. No. 82 triangular bon bon in teal
385. No. 82 triangular bon bon in blue

BOWLS AND COMPOTES

386 - 390. No. 68 Carltec 6" footed compotes

391. No. 83 Carltec 7" oblong bowl

392. No. 130 Martec footed jelly

393 - 394. No. 83 Carltec 7" oblong bowls

395 - 400. No. 130 Martec footed jellies

TABLEWARE

401. No. 312 Moon & Star Variant candlestick
402. No. 307 Moon & Star Variant footed compote
403. No. 312 Moon & Star Variant candlestick
404. No. 309 footed 11" cake stand
405. No. 131 Wiltec footed jelly
406. No. 65 Wiltec footed vase
407. No. 103 Wiltec Shamrock olive tray
408 - 410. No. 197 Valtec footed compotes
411. No. 159 Sextec salt & pepper
412. No. 124 Sextec covered butter
413. No. 61 Sextec goblet in amberina
414 - 415. Toltec whimseys

416. No. 126 Toltec celery or vase
417. No. 172 Sextec creamer
418. No. 173 Sextec sugar
419. No. 69 Sextec footed jelly
420. No. 214 Toltec creamer
421. No. 213 Toltec sugar
422. No. 71 Toltec oval footed nut bowl
423. No. 81 Toltec footed jelly
424. No. 208 Toltec footed toothpick
425. No. 167 Rotec creamer
426. No. 160 Rotec salt & pepper

YUTEC

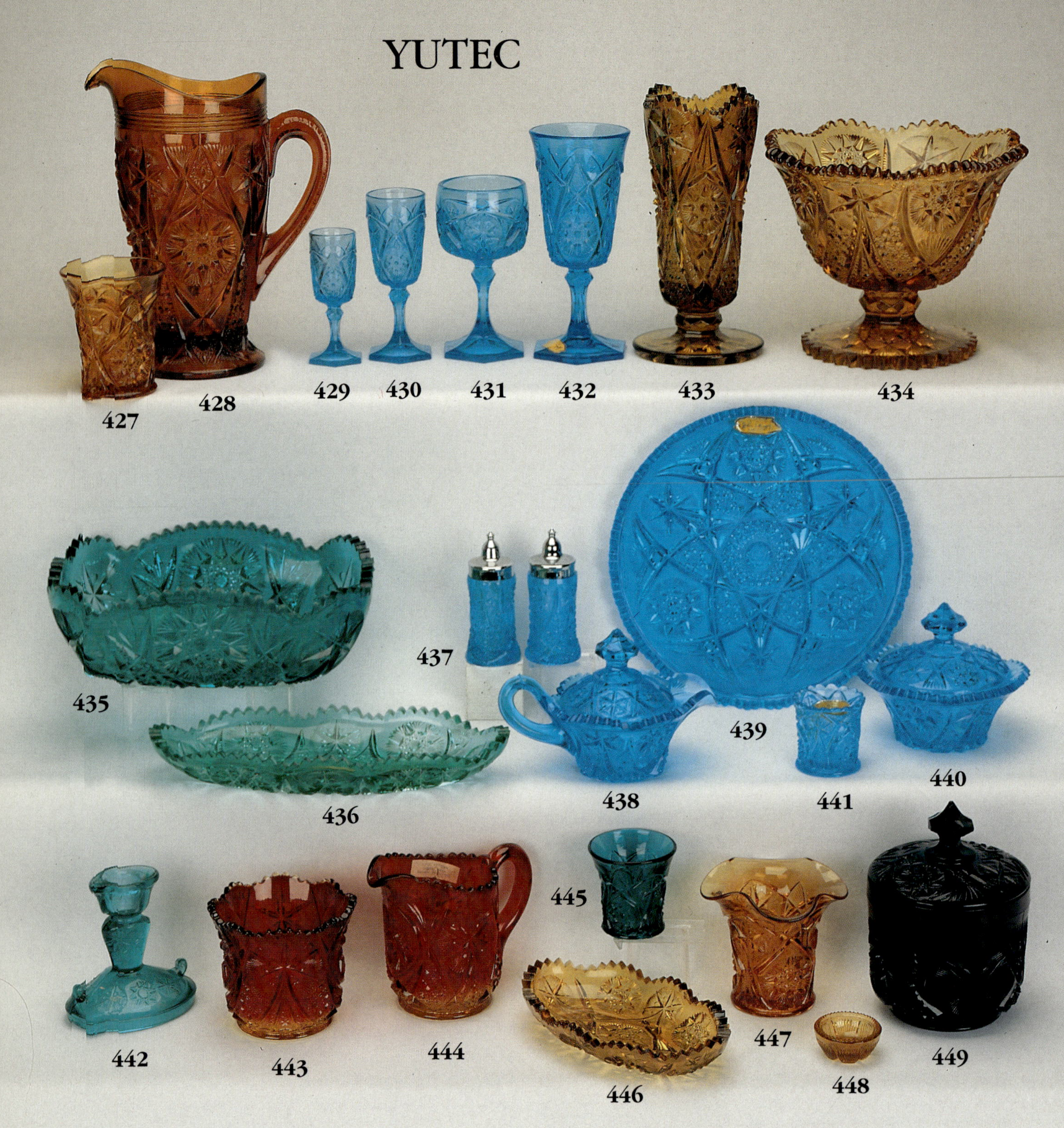

NO. 61 SEXTEC GOBLET

450. amber
451. dark green
452. milk glass
453. amberina
454. light amethyst

455. blue
456. light amber
457. green
458. dark amethyst

LACE & DEWDROP

459

460

461

462

463

464

465

466

467

468

469

470

471

472

473

474

459. No. 419 tall footed celery
460. No. 415 covered 6" compote
461. No. 419 tall footed celery
462. No. 409 water pitcher 36 oz.
463. No. 429 small hat
464. No. 425 small crimped vase

465 - 466. No. 426 small basket vases
467 - 471. No. 408 goblets 8 oz.
472. No. 418 large, crimped basket vase
473. No. 414 covered butter with flat finial
474. No. 412 sherbet

WHIMSEYS AND MISCELLANY

475. No. 111 Haley's Compote
476. unfinished stopper or knock-off
477. No. 275 Cherub plaque
478. No. 23 Lincoln Split Rail oval plaque
479. No. 56 Pillar Variant covered wedding jar
480. No. 151 V-Cane & Daisy 12 oz. ice tea

481. No. 66 Quintec footed vase
482. Optic pitcher
483. No. 239 Fish, free hand
484. free hand clown
485. No. 101 Westward Ho goblet
486. No. 81 Toltec footed jelly
487. No. 627 Yutec cruet
488. No. 249 Rex Variant mustard jar with cover

489. No. 247A Banzantine sugar
490. Banzantine footed jelly
491. 2-handled nappy
492. No. 292 Leaning ash tray
493. Optic goblet/vase
494. No. 66A Quintec salt & pepper
495. free hand ash tray
496. No. 239 Fish ivy holder, free hand

ASH TRAYS, BOXES AND SALTS

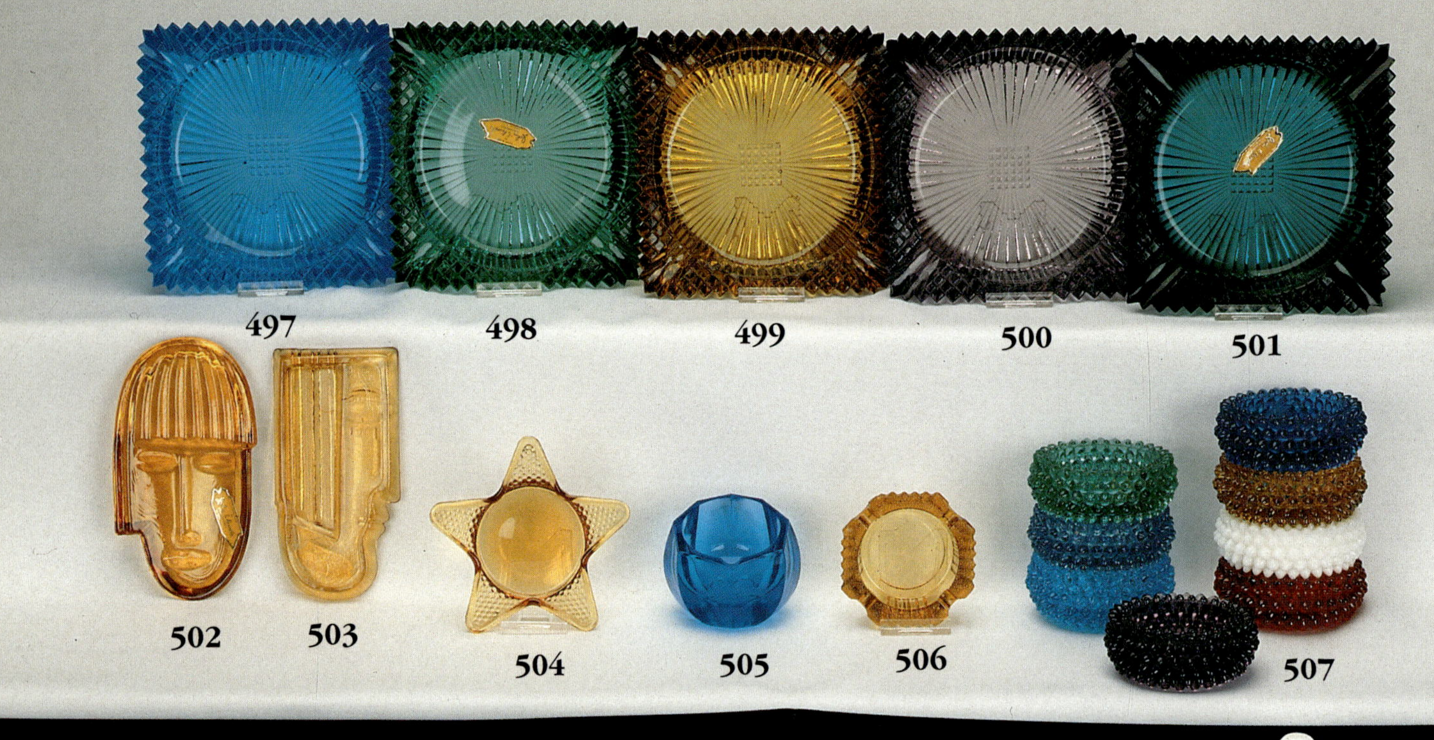

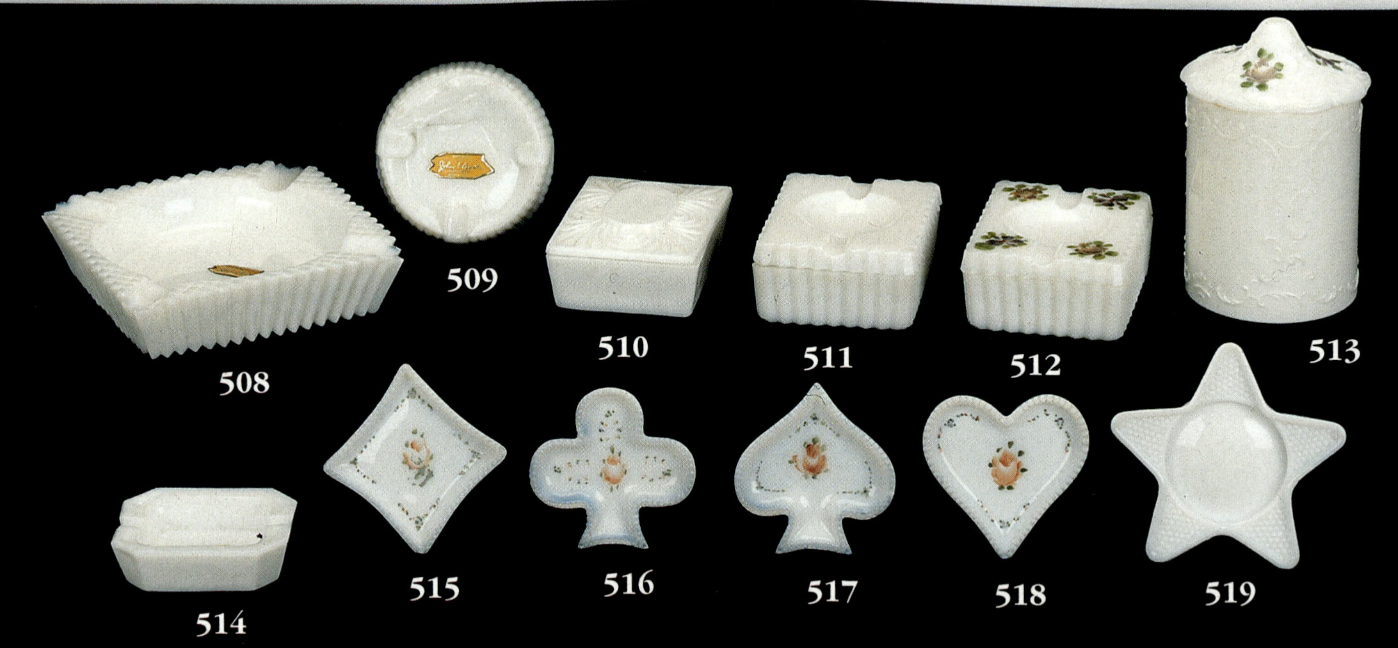

497. No. 90 Ribbed 6" square ash tray in blue
498. No. 90 Ribbed 6" square ash tray in green
499. No. 90 Ribbed 6" square ash tray in amber
500. No. 90 Ribbed 6" square ash tray in amethyst
501. No. 90 Ribbed 6" square ash tray in teal
502. No. 260B Cleopatra ash tray
503. No. 260A Caesar ash tray
504. No. 272 Star with Tear Drops ash tray
505. No. 292 Leaning ash tray
506. No. 3 Octagonal $2^1/_2$" x $2^1/_2$" ash tray
507. No. 67 Hobnail round master salts

508. No. 90 Ribbed 6" square ash tray
509. Ribbed 3-slot ash tray
510. No. 155 Versailles covered dresser box
511 - 512. No. 10 Rib Base cigarette boxes
with ash tray tops
513. No. 39 Scroll Variant covered cigar jar
514. No. 10-A Plain 2-slot oblong ash tray
515 - 518. No. 274 Diamond, Club, Spade, Heart
3" playing card ash trays
519. No. 272 Star with Tear Drops ash tray

BOWLS, COMPOTES AND TABLEWARE

520. No. 115 Sunburst 7¹/₂" footed compote
521. No. 118 Sunburst 8¹/₂" compote
522. No. 127 Sunburst footed compote
523. No. 141 Jubilee flared 6" vase
524. Jubilee 4" vase
525. No. 163 Jubilee flared 8" vase
526 - 528. No. 129 V-Cane & Daisy (Innovation Cut) 8"
     nut bowls in blue, amber, and green

529. No. 152 V-Cane & Daisy (Innovation) 8 oz. tumbler
530. No. 100 V-Cane & Daisy (Innovation Cut) sherbet
531. No. 161 Sunburst salt & pepper
532. No. 46 Sunburst 2-handle bon bon
533. No. 63 Sunburst celery or ivy vase
534. No. 88 Canoe (Innovation Cut) celery tray in blue
535. No. 88 Canoe (Innovation Cut) celery tray in green

INNOVATION CUT — CANE BAND & ROSE

536. No. 89 fruit bowl on No. 93 compote base 6", in blue
537. No. 89 fruit bowl on No. 93 compote base 6", in green
538. No. 89 fruit bowl on No. 93 compote base 6", in amber
539. No. 89 fruit bowl on No. 93 compote base 6", in milk glass
540. No. 150 4-toed oblong orange bowl

INNOVATION CUT — CANE BAND & ROSE

541

542

543

544

545

541. No. 86 Cane Band & Rose Napoleon's Hat banana boat on No. 93 compote base 6", amber
542. No. 86 Cane Band & Rose Napoleon's Hat banana boat on No. 93 compote base 6", green
543. No. 86 Cane Band & Rose Napoleon's Hat banana boat on No. 93 compote base 6", amberina
544. No. 86 Cane Band & Rose Napoleon's Hat banana boat on No. 93 compote base 6", milk glass
545. No. 86 Cane Band & Rose Napoleon's Hat banana boat on No. 93 compote base 6", blue

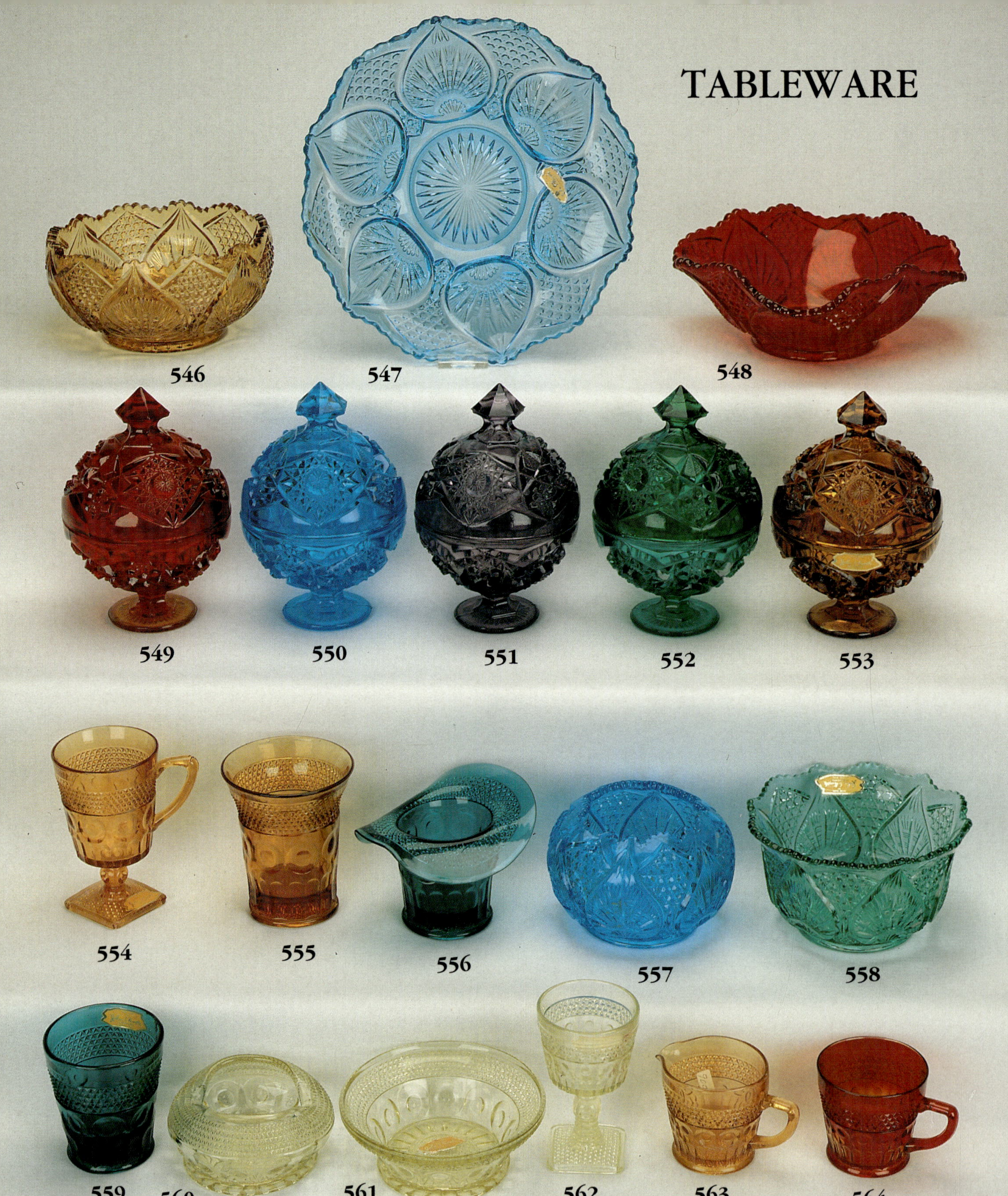

TABLEWARE

546. No. 72 Plytec 7" bowl
547. Plytec plate
548. No. 72/1 Plytec crimped 7" bowl
549 - 553. No. 49 Hobstar & Fan covered ftd. candies
554. No. 189 Sandwich mug
555. No. 184 Sandwich ice tea

556. No. 184 Sandwich whimsey
557. Plytec No. 60/2 rose bowl 6"
558. No. 74/1 Plytec 6½" crimped bowl
559 - 564. Sandwich No. 188 tumbler, rose bowl, open bowl, No. 186 tall sherbet, No. 191 creamer, and No. 189 mug

CANDLESTICKS

565. No. 198 Panel finger
566. No. 199 Yutec
567. No. 193 Eiffel Tower - Victor
568. No. 264A Bell base 10" Crucifix
569. No. 263 Floral base 7$\frac{1}{2}$" Crucifix

570 - 571. No. 420 Lace & Dewdrop 4$\frac{1}{2}$"
572 - 580. No. 40 Sawtooth
581 - 585. No. 70 Toltec oval footed
586 - 587. 3-footed
588. No. 312 Moon & Star Variant 3-footed
589 - 590. No. 94 Narcissus

WHIMSEYS

591. Martec stretched vase
592. Yutec goblet
593. Rotec swung vase or celery
594. Toltec whimsey vase
595. unidentified stretched vase
596. Carltec stretched vase
597. unidentified stretched vase
598. Yutec goblet

599. Martec crimped goblet
600. Toltec whimsey vase
601. Plytec whimsey spooner
602. Plytec whimsey spooner
603. unidentified swung vase
604 - 605. Aztec stretched spooners
606 - 607. stretched candle holders
608. Aztec stretched spooner

609. Yutec whimsey goblet
610. Lace & Dewdrop swung vase
611. Indian Chief toothpick
612. Yutec salt or pepper
613. Yutec salt or pepper
614. Yutec stretched salt or pepper
615. unidentified whimsey
616. Yutec whimsey toothpick

ANIMAL FIGURINES

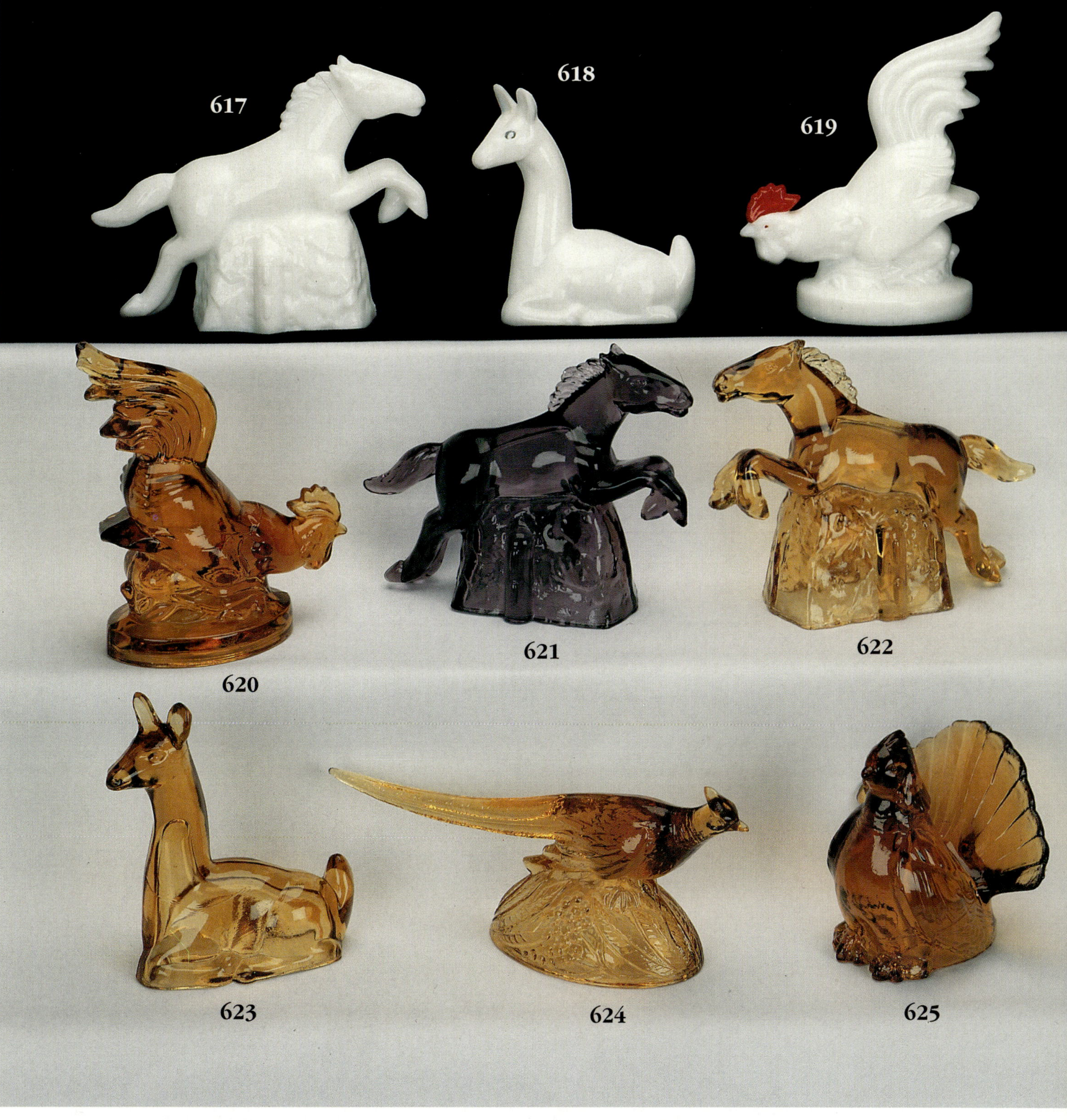

617. No. 253 Jumping Horse bookend in milk glass
618. No. 251 Deer (Llama) in milk glass
619. No. 244 Fighting Cock bookend in milk glass
620. No. 244 Fighting Cock bookend in amber
621. No. 253 Jumping Horse bookend in amethyst

622. No. 253 Jumping Horse bookend in amber
623. No. 251 Deer (Llama) in amber
624. No. 252 Pheasant in amber
625. No. 254 Grouse in amber

NO. 59 DOLPHIN DISH

626

627

628

629

630

631

632

633

634

635

636

637

626. blue
627. amberina
628. light amethyst
629. teal
630. light green

631. End-of-Day
632. West Virginia Red
633. amber
634. dark amethyst
635. blue

636. milk glass (a sticker inside its
mouth reads: "DOLPHIN Original
Mouth Greentown, Indiana—
1901.")
637. No. 266 Diamond Shell spoon

5½" ANIMALS ON NEST

638   639   640   641

642   643   644

645   646

638. No. 9 Lamb on split-rib base, blue

639. No. 1 Hen on split-rib base, amberina

640. No. 4 Rooster on split-rib base, amberina

641. No. 26 Rabbit on split-rib base, amber

642. No. 20 Turkey on split-rib base, light amethyst

643. No. 25 Cat on split-rib base, green

644. No. 36 Horse on split-rib base, dark amethyst

645. No. 4 Rooster on split-rib base, milk glass

646. No. 1 Hen on split-rib base, milk glass

7¹/₂" ANIMALS ON NEST

647

648

649

650

651

652

653

647. No. 24 Rooster on basket-weave base, green

648. No. 31 Hen on basketweave base, green

649. No. 15 Fox on basketweave base, amber

650. No. 33 Cow on basketweave base, black amethyst

651. No. 35 Lion on basketweave base, blue

652. No. 31 Hen on basketweave base, milk glass

653. No. 24 Rooster on basket-weave base, milk glass

BOTTLES, CRUETS AND VASES

654. No. 651 Sunburn cruet
655. No. 596 Optic tall flare vase with rigaree
656. No. 513 Rainbow bottle with stopper
657. No. 511/1 Rainbow vase
658. No. 508 Rib Base decanter with stopper and handle
659. No. 561 Optic tall vase w/leaf

660. No. 515 Lacey Heart vase
661. No. 555 Optic bulbous vase
662. No. 625 Yutec ewer w/handle
663. No. 603-SS Optic bottle with stopper
664. No. 504 Toltec decanter
665. No. 622 Optic swirl vase
666. No. 578-S Optic vase
667. Optic bulbous ewer
668. No. 555 Optic bulbous vase

669. No. 552 champion Petticoat cruet
670. No. 573-H Optic ewer
671. No. 589 Optic
672. Optic pitcher
673. No. 528 Petticoat vase
674. No. 557 Natural Crackle bottle with stopper
675. Optic vase whimsey
676. No. 606 Swirl ewer

BOTTLES, CRUETS AND VASES

677. No. 568 Pinched Optic bulbous decanter
678. No. 622 Optic Swirl vase
679. No. 581 Optic vase w/ruffle
680. Optic decanter
681. No. 639 Nat. Crackle pitcher
682. Optic pitcher
683. Optic ewer
684. No. 651 Sunburn cruet

685. Splatter pitcher
686. No. 660 Sunburst vase
687. No. 571-HS Optic decanter
688. No. 662 Sunburst bottle with stopper
689. No. 662 Sunburst bottle
690 - 692. Optic whimseys
693 - 694. No. 661 Sunburst lazy joes or ewers

695. No. 526 Champion cruet
696. No. 528 Champion vase
697. No. 528/1 Champion vase with wide mouth
698. No. 552 Champion Petticoat cruet (only)
699. No. 526 Plutec cruet
700. No. 528 Champion vase
701. No. 529 Champion ewer

GRAY ASSORTMENT

702. No. 89 Cane Band & Rose bowl on No. 130 Martec footed jelly base
703. No. 102-A Yutec 3 oz. cocktail
704. No. 408 Lace & Dewdrop 8 oz. goblet
705. No. 409 Lace & Dewdrop 36 oz. pitcher
706. No. 100 V-Cane & Daisy footed sherbet
707. No. 97 Yutec Chalice
708. No. 139 Yutec open sugar or spooner
709. No. 140 Yutec creamer
710. No. 69 Sextec footed jelly
711. No. 72 Plytec 7" bowl
712. No. 49 Hobstar & Fan covered candy dish

713. No. 197 Valtec footed compote
714. No. 178 Indian Chief toothpick
715. No. 137 Yutec salt & pepper
716. No. 71 Toltec oval footed nut bowl
717. No. 86 Napoleon's Hat Banana Boat on No. 69 Sextec footed jelly base
718. No. 415 Lace & Dewdrop 6" covered compote
719. No. 62 Aztec footed bon bon
720. No. 82 Bontec triangular bon bon
721. No. 31 Hen on Nest 7$\frac{1}{2}$" covered animal dish
722. No. 133 Yutec covered sugar
723. No. 136 Yutec covered creamer

717

718

719

720

721

722

723

Mrs. Kemple tells us the story behind this unique glass:

The secret recipe for the Kemple Glass Works' white milk glass was well-guarded by John and Geraldine Kemple. In 1964, during a period when John and Geraldine were both ill, none of the other workers knew how to mix the batch of milk glass that was needed for a particular day's run. They tried their best to combine the necessary ingredients and mix a batch themselves. The first few pieces came out of the furnace a milky gray color, a far cry from the smooth white they were meant to be.

Eventually, John and Geraldine discovered the mistake and several of these miscolored pieces were dumped behind the factory with the other waste. However John did salvage the majority of the batch, taking the pieces to Cincinnati, OH to be sold.

Somehow, 27 pieces ended up in the shop of a collector in Louisville, KY. In 1974 or 1975, another collector from Huntington, WV visited the Louisville shop and purchased those pieces. Shortly afterwards, co-author John Burkholder tracked down the gray milk glass and purchased the entire set for a good sum of money. To our knowledge, none of the gray milk pieces had ever been marketed by the Kemple Glass Works, and if any exist other than those in the Burkholder collection, they are extremely rare.

724. No. 62 Aztec footed bon bon
725 - 726. No. 40 Sawtooth candlesticks
727. No. 93 Cane Band & Rose 6" compote
728. No. 4 Rooster on Nest 5$\frac{1}{2}$" covered animal dish
729. No. 175 Waffle & Button miniature covered sugar
730. No. 59 Dolphin dish with fish finial
731 - 732. No. 20 Turkey on Nest 5$\frac{1}{2}$" covered animal dishes

733. No. 208 Toltec footed toothpick
734. No. 36 Horse on Nest 5$\frac{1}{2}$" covered animal dish
735. No. 276 Scroll Variant toothpick
736. No. 4 Rooster on Nest 5$\frac{1}{2}$" covered animal dish
737. No. 32 Puss-in-Boots slipper
738. No. 51 Lace & Dewdrop covered peanut jar
739. No. 213 Toltec sugar
740. No. 214 Toltec creamer

END-OF-DAY ASSORTMENT

741. No. 89 Cane Band & Rose compote on No. 130 Martec footed jelly base

742. No. 31 Hen on Nest 7¹/₂" covered animal dish

743. No. 97 Yutec chalice

744. No. 106 Yutec 10" oblong fruit bowl

745. No. 72 Plytec 7" bowl

746. No. 24 Rooster on Nest 7¹/₂" covered animal dish

747. No. 74 Plytec 6¹/₂" bowl

748. Lace & Dewdrop tall sugar with cover

749. No. 93 Cane Band & Rose 6" compote
750. No. 21 Chick egg cup
751. No. 81 Toltec footed jelly
752. No. 209 Lincoln Hat (Waffle Hat) toothpick
753. No. 145 Aztec covered sugar or candy
754. No. 36 Horse 5½" covered animal dish
755. No. 4 Rooster on Nest 5½" covered animal dish
756. No. 1 Hen on Nest 5½" covered animal dish
757. No. 36 Horse 5½" covered animal dish

758. No. 414 Lace & Dewdrop covered butter
759. No. 20 Turkey 5½" covered animal dish
760. No. 27 Helping Hand ash tray
761. No. 414 Lace & Dewdrop covered butter
762. No. 162 Basket 2-handled toothpick
763. No. 428 Lace & Dewdrop low open sugar
764. No. 427 Lace & Dewdrop low creamer
765. No. 177 Waffle & Button covered butter

766   767   768   769

770   771   772   773

WEST VIRGINIA RED (1963 CENTENNIAL)

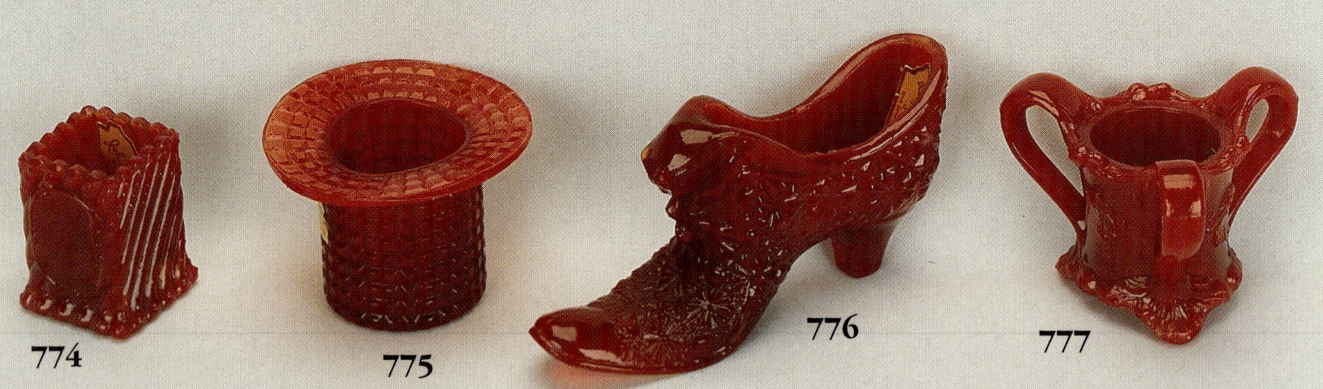

774   775   776   777

766. No. 242 Gypsy Kettle ash tray
767. No. 47 Trunk treasure chest
768. No. 130 Martec footed jelly
769. No. 208 Toltec footed toothpick
770. No. 59 Dolphin dish with fish finial
771. No. 177 Waffle & Button covered butter

772. No. 175 Waffle & Button covered sugar
773. No. 176 Waffle & Button creamer
774. No. 277 Scroll Variant toothpick
775. No. 209 Lincoln Hat (Waffle Hat) toothpick
776. No. 32 Puss-in-Boots slipper
777. No. 5 Pansy Flower toothpick

CHALICE, LAMPS AND VASE

778

779

780

781

782

783

784

785

786

787

778. No. 97 Yutec chalice in End-of-Day

779. No. 50 Art Dressed cameo triangular vase, milk glass

780. No. 97 Yutec chalice in West Va. Centennial Red

781 - 787. Assorted lamp bases in milk glass, No. 297 and No. 350

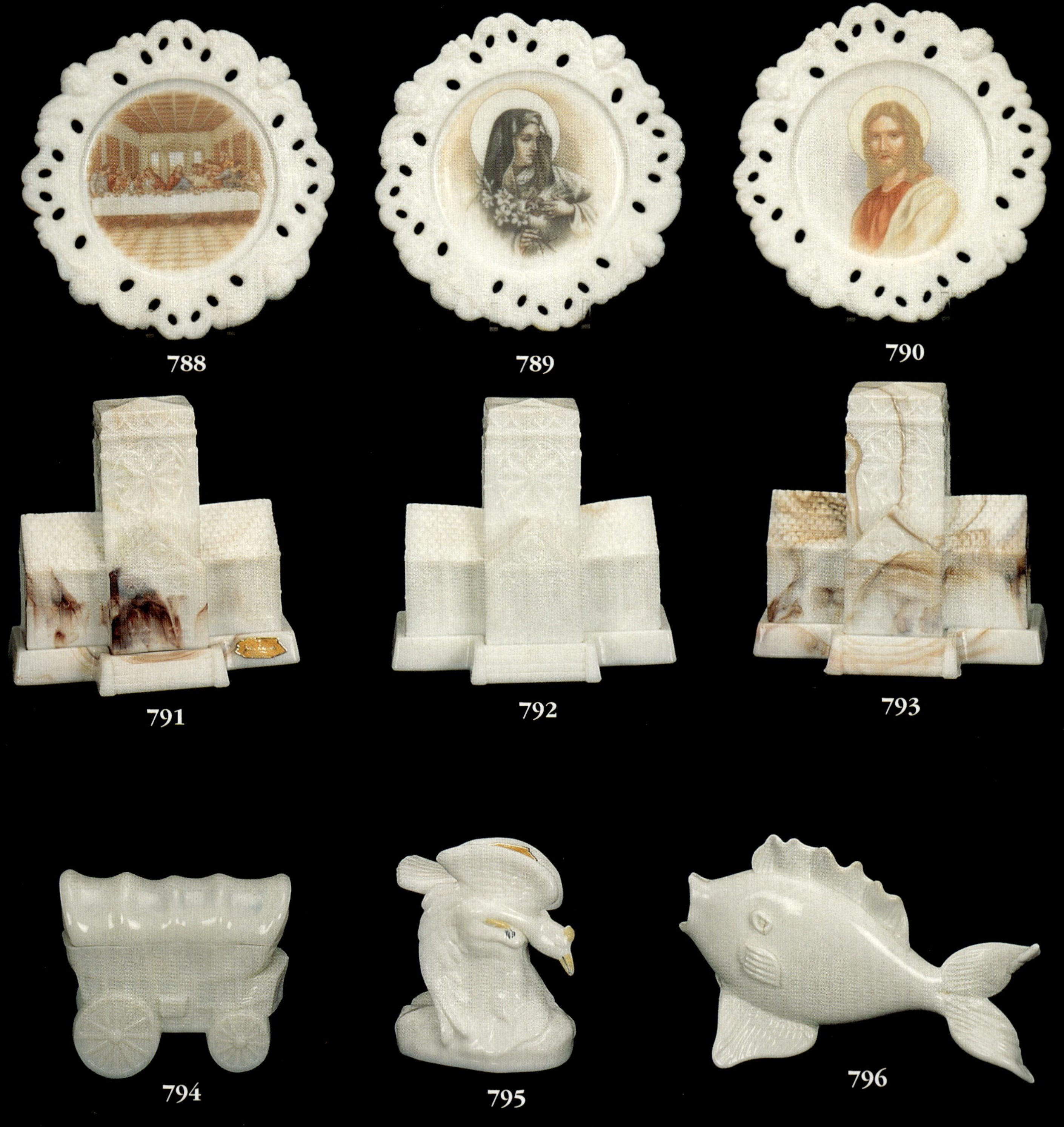

788

789

790

791

792

793

794

795

796

788. No. 29 Angel Head 8$\frac{1}{2}$" plate—Lord's Supper

789. No. 29 Angel Head 8$\frac{1}{2}$" plate—Mary

790. No. 29 Angel Head 8$\frac{1}{2}$" plate—Christ

791. No. 284 Church lamp in End-of-Day

792. No. 284 Church lamp in milk glass

793. No. 284 Church lamp in End-of-Day

794. No. 255 Stage Coach figurine in milk glass

795. No. 241 Bird of Paradise figurine in milk glass

796. No. 239 Fish free hand ivy holder in milk glass

KEMPLE GLASS IN COLOR
CATALOG PAGE REPRINTS

The next section illustrates color catalog page reprints from a 1960s Kemple Glass Works catalog. The items shown were produced by Kemple Glass while at the Kenova factory. On some of the following pages (95 - 105) the reader can find slogans such as "Kemple—A name known in glass for over 85 years" or "Authentic Antique Reproductions Processed By Hand In The Original Old Molds." Underneath each item appears Kemple's catalog number, usually beginning with a color code (FR or GR for amberina, ED for End-of-Day, B for blue, no code for milk glass, etc.). All pieces with Kemple catalog numbers can be easily identified in the Item Number Index beginning on page 137.

Included at the end of this section (pp. 106 - 112) are color flyers of Wheatonware and Wheatoncraft items. The pieces are identified by Wheatoncraft item number, however we have included descriptions below each flyer using the corresponding Kemple item number.

FR40. No. 40 Sawtooth candlesticks	**ED49.** No. 49 Hobstar & Fan covered footed candy
FR68. No. 68 Carltec footed compote	**ED81.** No. 81 Toltec footed jelly
FR115. No. 115 Sunburst 7½" footed compote	**ED4.** No. 4 Hen on Nest covered animal dish on 5½" split-rib base
FR97. No. 97 Yutec chalice	
FR197. No. 197 Valtec footed compote	**ED59.** No. 59 Dolphin dish
FR62. No. 62 Aztec footed bon bon	**ED36.** No. 36 Horse covered animal dish on 5½" split-rib base
FR145. No. 145 Aztec covered sugar or candy	
FR49. No. 49 Hobstar & Fan covered footed candy	**ED20.** No. 20 Turkey covered animal dish on 5½" split-rib base
ED93. No. 93 Cane Band & Rose 6" compote	

Kemple Glass

Authentic Antique Reproductions

"A name known in glass for over 85 years"

GR62. No. 62 Aztec footed bon bon

GR49. No. 49 Hobstar & Fan covered candy dish

GR69. No. 69 Sextec footed jelly

GR63. No. 63 Sunburst vase

GR130. No. 130 Martec footed jelly

GR40. No. 40 Sawtooth candlesticks

GR66. No. 66 Quintec footed vase

GR197. No. 197 Valtec ftd. compote

GR408. No. 408 Lace & Dewdrop 8 oz. goblet

GR70. No. 70 Toltec candlesticks

GR93. No. 93 Cane Band & Rose 6" compote

GR139. No. 139 Yutec open sugar

96

Top row: No. 115 Sunburst 7$^{1}/_{2}$" footed compote; No. 97 Yutec chalice; No. 244 Fighting Cock figurine; No. 29 Angel Head 8$^{1}/_{2}$" plate; No. 409 Lace & Dewdrop 36 oz. water pitcher. **Second row:** No. 72/C Plytec crimped bowl; No. 4 Rooster on Nest 5$^{1}/_{2}$" covered animal dish; No. 78 Aztec 7" covered butter; No. 137 Yutec salt & pepper; No. 402 Lace & Dewdrop covered bowl. **Third row:** No. 8 Cabbage Rose round dresser box; No. 48 Lion Head dresser box; No. 50 Lion Head round dresser box; No. 208/1 Toltec footed toothpick; No. 197 Valtec footed compote; No. 130 Martec footed jelly; No. 18 Scroll with Fleur de Lis dresser box. **Fourth row:** No. 408 Lace & Dewdrop 8 oz. goblet; No. 94 Narcissus candlesticks; No. 31 Hen 7$^{1}/_{2}$" covered animal dish. **Bottom row:** No. 96 Cane Band & Rose Napoleon's Hat bowl on compote; No. 133 Yutec covered sugar; No. 136 Yutec covered creamer; No. 70 Toltec oval footed candlesticks.

Top row: No. 66 Quintec ftd. vase; No. 49 Hobstar & Fan footed candy dish; No. 159 Sextec salt & pepper; No. 59 Dolphin dish with fish finial. **Second row:** No. 132 V-Cane & Daisy 8 oz. tumbler; No. 77-A Bontec boat-shaped bon bon; No. 5 Pansy Flower 3-handled toothpick; No. 83 Carltec 7" oblong bowl. **Third row:** No. 133 Yutec covered candy; No. 151 V-Cane & Daisy 12 oz. ice tea; No. 20 Turkey 5$\frac{1}{2}$" covered animal dish. **Bottom row:** No. 103 Wiltec Shamrock olive tray; No. 32 Puss-in-Boots slipper; No. 89 Cane Band & Rose fruit bowl on compote base.

Kemple Glass

Top row: No. 62 Aztec footed bon bon; No. 70 Toltec oval footed candlestick; No. 86 Cane Band & Rose Napoleon's Hat banana boat on compote base (here displayed holding a floral arrangement); No. 46 Sunburst 2-handled bon bon. **Second row:** No. 85 Aztec spooner; No. 84 Aztec creamer; No. 159 Sextec salt & pepper; No. 173 Sextec sugar; No. 172 Sextec creamer; No. 168 Rotec 2-handled sugar; No. 167 Rotec creamer. **Third row:** No. 199 Yutec candlesticks; No. 94 Narcissus candlesticks; No. 74 Plytec 6 1/2" bowl; No. 198 Panel finger candlesticks; No. 72 Plytec 7" crimped bowl. **Bottom row:** No. 88 Innovation—Canoe 13" celery tray; No. 135 Yutec 7" low bowl; No. 99 Bontec handled heart bon bon; No. 83 Carltec 7" oblong bowl.

Kemple Glass

"A name known in glass for over 85 years"

Authenic Antique Reproduction Pattern Glass, Processed by hand in the original old molds.
Colors: Honey Amber, Blue, Amethyst and Milk glass.

Top row: No. 197 Valtec footed compote in amethyst, milk glass, blue, and honey amber. **Second row:** No. 69 Sextec footed jelly in honey amber and milk glass; No. 93 Cane Band & Rose 6" compote in blue, milk glass, and honey amber; No. 130 Martec footed jelly in blue and amethyst. **Third row:** No. 69 Sextec footed jelly in amethyst and blue; No. 49 Hobstar & Fan covered candy dish in amethyst, milk glass, blue, and honey amber; No. 130 Martec footed jelly in milk glass and honey amber. **Fourth row:** No. 133 Yutec covered sugar in honey amber and amethyst; No. 145 Aztec covered sugar in honey amber and amethyst. **Bottom row:** No. 133 Yutec covered sugar in blue and milk glass; No. 97 Yutec chalice in honey amber, blue, milk glass, and amethyst; No. 145 Aztec covered sugar in milk glass and blue.

Top row: No. 4 Rooster on Nest 5¹/₂" covered animal dish in amethyst, blue, milk glass, and honey amber.
Second row: No. 25 Cat 5¹/₂" covered animal dish in honey amber, milk glass, blue, and light amethyst.
Third row: No. 9 Lamb 5¹/₂" covered animal dish in light amethyst, blue, milk glass, and honey amber.
Fourth row: No. 1 Hen on Nest 5¹/₂" covered animal dish in honey amber, milk glass, blue, and amethyst.
Fifth row: No. 36 Horse 5¹/₂" covered animal dish in light amethyst, blue, milk glass, and honey amber.
Bottom row: No. 20 Turkey 5¹/₂" covered animal dish in honey amber, milk glass, blue, and amethyst.

Top row: No. 89 Cane Band & Rose fruit bowl on compote base; No. 101 Westward Ho—Deer & Buffalo goblet; No. 61 Sextec goblet; No. 195 Aztec 9 oz. goblet; No. 118 Sunburst 8½" footed compote. **Second row:** No. 33 Cow 7½" covered animal dish; No. 35 Lion 7½" covered animal dish; No. 15 Fox 7½" covered animal dish; No. 24 Rooster on Nest 7½" covered animal dish; No. 31 Hen on Nest 7½" covered animal dish. **Third row:** No. 129 V-Cane & Daisy 8" nut bowl; No. 100 V-Cane & Daisy footed sherbet; No. 134 Yutec condiment tray; No. 117 Yutec 10¼" celery tray; No. 90 Ribbed 6" square ash tray. **Bottom row:** No. 408 Lace & Dewdrop 8 oz. goblet; No. 409 Lace & Dewdrop 36 oz. water pitcher; No. 159 Sextec salt & pepper; No. 160 Rotec salt & pepper; No. 137 Yutec salt & pepper; No. 108 Yutec covered sugar; No. 71 Toltec oval footed nut bowl; No. 123 Yutec tumbler; No. 128 Yutec water pitcher.

The following assortment is shown in amethyst, blue, honey amber, and milk glass. **Top row:** No. 122 Yutec toothpick; No. 206 Pony & Cart toothpick. **Second row:** No. 178 Indian Chief toothpick; No. 5 Pansy Flower toothpick. **Third row:** No. 175 Waffle & Button covered sugar; No. 32 Puss-in-Boots slipper. **Fourth row:** No. 210 Coal Bucket with Bail ash tray; No. 176 Waffle & Button creamer. **Fifth row:** No. 245 Basket Weave toothpick; No. 208 footed toothpick. **Bottom row:** No. 67 Hobnail round master salt; No. 242 Gypsy Kettle ash tray; No. 242 Gypsy Kettle toothpick.

This assortment is shown in amethyst, blue, honey amber, and milk glass. **Top row:** No. 40 Sawtooth candlesticks; No. 115 Sunburst 7¹⁄₂" footed compote. **Second row:** No. 40 Sawtooth candlesticks; No. 59 Dolphin dish with fish finial. **Third row:** No. 78 Aztec 7" covered butter; No. 130 Martec footed jelly. **Fourth row:** No. 124 Sextec covered butter; No. 139 Yutec open sugar or spooner; No. 140 Yutec creamer. **Fifth row:** No. 103 Wiltec Shamrock olive tray; No. 82 Bontec triangular bon bon; No. 133 Yutec covered sugar; No. 136 Yutec covered creamer. **Bottom row:** No. 103 Wiltec Shamrock olive tray; No. 82 Bontec triangular bon bon; No. 133 Yutec covered sugar; No. 136 Yutec covered creamer.

104

Top row: No. 62/C Aztec crimped compote; No. 69 Sextec footed jelly; No. 93 Cane Band & Rose 6" compote; No. 145 Aztec covered sugar; No. 145/C Aztec fluted bon bon. **Second row:** No. 206 Pony & Cart toothpick; No. 121 Yutec 4½" round nappy; No. 242/243 (incorrectly labeled 245/243) Gypsy Kettle toothpick and ash tray; No. 117 Yutec 10¼" celery tray; No. 1 Hen on Nest 5½" covered animal dish. **Third row:** No. 25 Cat 5½" covered animal dish; No. 16-B Lacy Heart 7½" plate; No. 99 Bontec handled heart bon bon; No. 122 Yutec toothpick; No. 40 Sawtooth candlesticks. **Fourth row:** No. 61 Sextec goblet; No. 82 Bontec triangular bon bon; No. 160 Rotec salt & pepper; No. 111 Haley's compote; No. 415 Lace & Dewdrop 6" compote. **Bottom row:** No. 129 V-Cane & Daisy 8" nut bowl; No. 67 Hobnail master salt; No. 75 Bontec 5" handled nappy; No. 106 Yutec 10" oblong bowl.

1., 8. No. 140 Yutec creamer
2., 9. No. 108 Yutec covered sugar
3. No. 307 Moon & Star Variant footed compote
4. No. 130 Martec footed jelly
5. No. 116 Yutec 7" covered butter
6 - 7. No. 40 Sawtooth candlesticks
10 - 11. No. 70 Toltec oval footed candlesticks
12 - 14. No. 198 Panel candlesticks
15. No. 94 Narcissus candlesticks
16. Swirl candlesticks

A. No. 307 Moon & Star Variant footed compote
B. No. 87 Cane Band & Rose Napoleon's Hat banana boat
C. No. 134 Yutec condiment tray
D. No. 19A/B Mary and Jesus plaques
E. No. 257 Colonial Lady figurine
F. No. 79 Valtec 5" handled nappy
G. No. 88 Innovation Cut Canoe tray
H. No. 256 Southern Belle figurine
I. No. 258 Victorian Lady figurine
J. No. 139 Yutec open sugar

K. Sheaf of Wheat plates
L. No. 59 Dolphin dish with fish finial
M. No. 103 Wiltec Shamrock olive tray
N. No. 49 Hobstar & Fan covered candy dish
O. No. 116 Yutec 7" covered butter
P. Yutec jelly
Q. No. 130 Martec footed jelly
R. No. 106 Yutec 10" oblong bowl
S - T. two miscellaneous paperweights

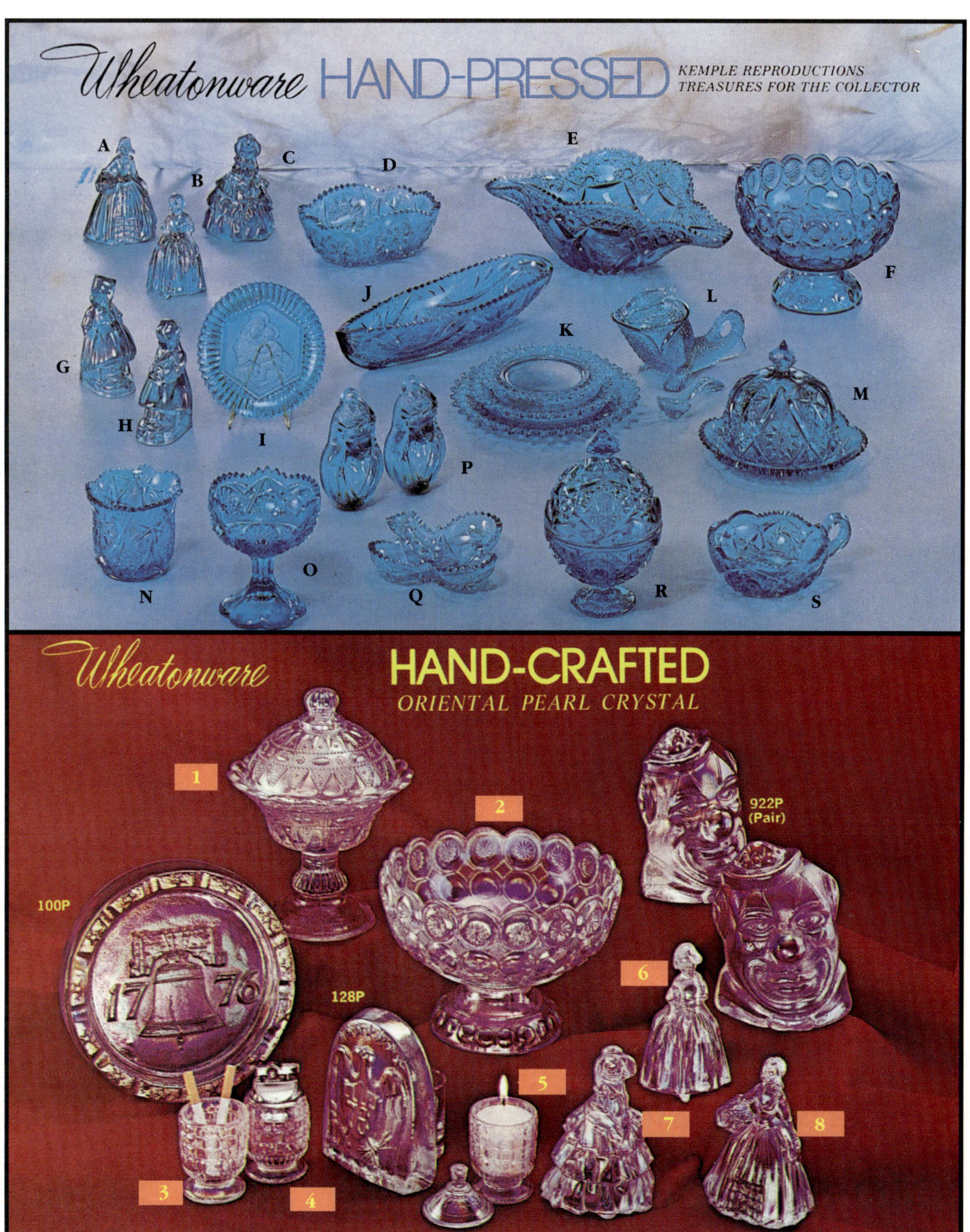

A. No. 257 Colonial Lady figurine
B. No. 258 Victorian Lady figurine
C. No. 256 Southern Belle figurine
D. Yutec jelly
E. No. 87 Cane Band & Rose Napoleon's Hat banana boat
F. No. 307 Moon & Star Variant footed compote
G - H. No. 259A/B Dutch Boy and Girl bookends
I. No. 993 Mary & Child 6" plate
J. No. 88 Innovation Cut Canoe tray

K. Sheaf of Wheat plates
L. No. 59 Dolphin dish w/fish finial
M. No. 116 Yutec 7" covered butter
N. No. 139 Yutec open sugar
O. No. 130 Martec footed jelly
P. No. 19A/B Mary and Jesus plaques
Q. No. 103 Wiltec Shamrock olive tray
R. No. 49 Hobstar & Fan covered candy dish
S. No. 79 Valtec 5" handled nappy

1. No. 415 Lace & Dewdrop 6" compote
2. No. 307 Moon & Star Variant footed compote
3 - 4. No. 174 Waffle & Button spooner
5. No. 175 Waffle & Button covered sugar
6. No. 258 Victorian Lady figurine
7. No. 256 Southern Belle figurine
8. No. 257 Colonial Lady figurine

Wheaton Industries came out with a line of place settings and tableware called Wheatoncraft. Unlike Wheatonware, Wheatoncraft was not sold through the home party plan but in retail stores and at the Wheaton Village gift shop. This 1976 assortment consists of a table setting in amber or blue, in the Lace & Dewdrop pattern: **296.** No. 415 compote 6"; **286.** No. 404 covered 6" bowl; **284.** No. 403-A covered 8" bowl; **276.** No. 408 water pitcher 36 oz.; **288.** No. 406 sauce 4"; **290.** 420 candlesticks 4$\frac{1}{2}$"; **280.** No. 414 covered butter w/flat finial; **278.** No. 427 creamer and No. 427 sugar; **254.** No. 424 cup; **256.** No. 423 saucer; **258.** No. 412 sherbet; **250.** No. 416 plate 10"; **252.** No. 403 plate 8"; **282.** No. 422 bowl 10"; **268.** No. 407 tumbler; **272.** No. 408 goblet.

This 1976 assortment displays the Moon & Star Variant, Lace & Dewdrop, and Pineapple patterns in crystal, amber, blue and green. The Moon & Star Variant compote serving as a vase is shown in Carnival glass, and the antique mold used to create this compote is pictured in the foreground.

296. No. 415 Lace & Dewdrop 6" compote
184. No. 46 Pineapple tall jelly
198. No. 307 Moon & Star Variant footed compote

154. No. 87 Cane Band & Rose Napoleon's Hat banana boat; **156.** No. 89 Cane Band & Rose orange bowl (without base); **202.** No. 134 Yutec condiment tray; **204.** No. 140 Yutec creamer; **176.** No. 139 Yutec open sugar; **152.** No. 130 Martec footed jelly; **170.** No. 119 Yutec 7" relish; **192.** No. 121 Yutec 4$\frac{1}{2}$" round nappy; **196.** No. 45 Hobstar & Fan covered butter; **172.** No. 106 Yutec 10" oblong bowl; **206.** No. 108 Yutec covered sugar; **150.** No. 49 Hobstar & Fan covered compote.

214. Swirl candleholders; **764.** No. 141 Jubilee 6" vase; **768.** No. 163 Jubilee 8" vase; **216.** No. 40 Sawtooth candlesticks; **212.** No. 70 Toltec oval footed candlesticks; **210.** No. 210 Panel finger candlesticks; **194.** No. 96 Aztec 6" handled nappy; **182, 180, 178.** Sheaf of Wheat plates; **218.** No. 94 Narcissus candlesticks; **188.** No. 136 Yutec covered sugar; **190.** No. 133 Yutec covered creamer; **290.** No. 420 Lace & Dewdrop 4¹/₂" candlesticks; **174.** No. 103 Wiltec Shamrock olive tray; **159.** No. 266 Diamond Shell mustard spoon; **158.** No. 59 Dolphin dish with fish finial; **744.** No. 993 Mary & Child 6" plate.

Lace & Dewdrop assortment in green, previously shown in amber and blue. **276.** No. 408 water pitcher 36 oz.; **258.** No. 412 sherbet; **252.** No. 403 plate 8"; **250.** No. 416 plate 10"; **254.** No. 424 cup; **256.** No. 423 saucer; **282.** No. 422 bowl 10"; **272.** No. 408 goblet; **268.** No. 407 tumbler; **288.** No. 406 sauce 4"; **278.** No. 427 creamer and No. 427 sugar; **280.** No. 414 covered butter w/flat finial; **286.** No. 404 covered 6" bowl; **296.** No. 415 compote 6"; **284.** No. 403-A covered 8" bowl; **290.** 420 candlesticks $4^1/_2$".

CHAPTER SIX
MISCELLANEOUS MOLD PURCHASES

In addition to the Mannington, Tuska, and McKee molds, Kemple also purchased molds from smaller companies and private individuals. Specifically, this chapter identifies the molds acquired from Kenneth R. Haley (American Glass Company), the Sinclair Glass Company of Ceredo, West Virginia, and from private owners. This chapter also covers miscellaneous pieces that were designed and made free hand (without molds) at the Kemple factory.

AMERICAN GLASS COMPANY

About 25 molds were purchased during the 1950s from the American Glass Company in Caney, Kansas. At first, we believed all these molds were bought in 1958. However, a photograph of the Kemple display at a circa 1950 trade show includes the Rooster or *Fighting Cock* bookend (illustrated on p. 114), a dramatic figural piece designed by Kenneth R. Haley for the American Glass Company.

According to Jack D. Wilson (*Phoenix & Consoli-*
dated Art Glass 1926-1980, pg. 8), Haley designed molds for many companies, even before he started the General Glassware Company in Greensburg, Pennsylvania. This firm was begun in partnership with Herman Lowerwitz of the American Glass Company of Caney, Kansas. American Glass did the actual glass manufacturing, and General Glassware was the distributor. When Lowerwitz died in 1946, the partnership was dissolved, and Haley started the K. R. Haley Glassware Company, Inc. also in Greensburg, that was in operation until 1972.

American Glass Company and K. R. Haley Glassware produced their wares in clear and milk glass. The Kemple reproductions were made in milk glass and, after 1958, in selected colors.

Wilson's book shows a photograph of K. R. Haley Glassware's sales brochure dated May 1, 1948 (pg. 178). The following pieces were featured in crystal and milk glass by K. R. Haley (Haley's names are listed first; Kemple's names are in parentheses): Horse and Cart (Kemple item No. 206 *Pony and Cart*); Conestoga Wagon box

K. R. Haley Glassware Company catalog (May 1, 1948), displaying pieces in milk glass whose molds would be later acquired by Kemple. Recognizable are the Haley's Compote, Pony & Cart, Covered Wagon box, Fighting Cock bookend, and the three Belle figurines. (*Phoenix & Consolidated Art Glass, 1926-1980*, p. 178.)

K. R. Haley's "Rooster," which the Kemples called the No. 244 Fighting Cock bookends.

The three lady figurines from American Glass Company: Colonial Lady with basket, Southern Belle with hat, and Victorian Lady. Made in milk glass, amber, and possibly other colors. Kemple Nos. 256 - 258.

The rare and charming Kemple No. 284 Church Lamp made at the Kenova factory, in milk glass, caramel slag, and a few pieces in blue slag. The April 1980 edition of *Glass Review* lists this item as originating from Consolidated Lamp and Shade Company, in Coraopolis, Pa., but our research lists the mold as an American Glass Company acquisition. This large shape was difficult to make. The roof on some pieces sagged during the annealing process.

Designed by K. R. Haley for American Glass Company, No. 111 "Haley's Compote," made in milk glass, amberina, and possibly other colors.

with cover (No. 255 *Stage Coach*); Rooster bookends (No. 244 *Fighting Cock*); and 5¹/₂" figurines called Lady (No. 256 *Southern Belle* with hat), Flower Girl (No. 258 *Victorian Lady* with basket), and Girl (No. 257 *Colonial Lady*). Other items, not pictured in the Haley ad but included among items Kemple produced from American Glass molds, are the No. 284 *Church Lamp*; No. 111 *Haley's* covered compote; No. 241 *Bird of Paradise* figurine; No. 259A and No. 259B *Dutch Boy and Dutch Girl* book-ends; No. 251-254 *Deer (Llama), Pheasant, Jumping Horse,* and *Grouse* figurines; and No. 292 whimsey *Leaning* ash tray.

Of the American Glass pieces, the following have been found in private collections in these colors (with other colors or color variations being possible): the Jumping Horse in milk glass, amber and amethyst; the Fighting Cock in milk glass and amber; the Deer (Llama) figurine in amber; the Pheasant in slag; the Bird of Paradise figurine in milk glass and amber; the Squatting Grouse in milk glass; the Pony and Cart in milk glass, amber, amethyst and blue; the Belle figurines in milk glass; and Haley's 5¹/₂" compote in milk glass and amberina. In some instances, Haley's Compote in milk glass had tiny, hand-painted flowers around the lid.

SINCLAIR GLASS COMPANY

The last significant set of molds purchased by Kemple Glass Works came from the Sinclair Glass Company, Ceredo, West Virginia, in late 1958. These 30 molds consisted mostly of ash trays, planters and small items. There were an assortment of patterns, many of which Sinclair Glass had purchased from other discontinued companies.

Various types of ash trays were included:
No. 3 2¹/₂" *Ribbed* four-slot octagonal
No. 10A *Plain* two-slot oblong
No. 11 *Triangle Scroll*

This Pony & Cart design—Kemple No. 206, purchased from American Glass Company, was used as an ash tray or toothpick.

No. 90 6" *Ribbed* four-slot square
No. 260A-B *Caesar* and *Cleopatra*
No. 261-262 *Horse and Indian*
No. 10 *Rib Base* oblong cigarette box w/ash tray top.
The No. 11, No. 90 and No. 975 ash trays are illustrated below.

Other Sinclair molds produced the following:
No. 973-975 *Open Edge* square cup, saucer, 8" plate
No. 54V set of *Plain*, hand-painted candlesticks
No. 53V *Plain*, hand-painted planter/napkin holder
No. 52-I 6" *Plain*, hand-painted bowl
No. 55-I *Plain*, hand-painted open sugar, creamer
No. 30 *Diamond & Rib* covered dresser box
No. 164 *Chain Link* and cigarette box
No. 165 *Plain Lid* cigarette box.

The series hand-painted with ivy leaves is listed with an "I", and pieces painted with violets, "V". These items were all made in milk glass. The Sinclair ash trays were reproduced primarily in milk glass as well, with the exception of the Ribbed pattern found in amber.

No. 11, Triangle Scroll ash tray, one of the Sinclair molds which Kemple produced in milk glass and various colors; No. 90, Ribbed pattern ash tray, in milk glass; the third piece in the Open Edge trio— 8" square plate, No. 975. The Ribbed pattern was prevalent in Sinclair's ash trays and cigarette box bases.

The John E. Kemple Glass Works at its factory site in Kenova, West Virginia.

An outlet store located on Rt. 60 and 12th St. in Kenova, West Virginia

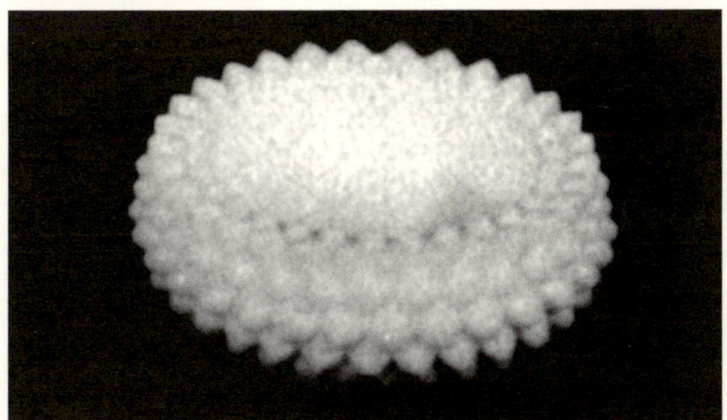

Kemple No. 67, the Hobnail master salt
purchased from Pete Zarilla.

Trunk Treasure Chest box, a Greentown acquisition,
Kemple No. 47, shown here in milk glass.

The Lincoln Split-Rail plaque, Kemple No. 23,
in milk glass.

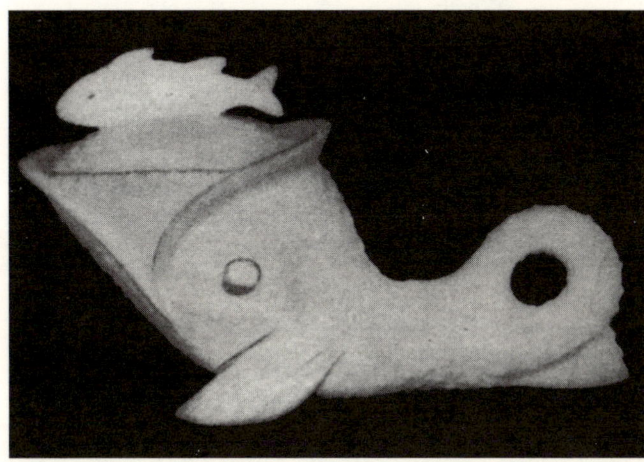

This Dolphin dish with fish finial cover became known as
Kemple No. 59. A Greentown piece, which Kemple purchased in 1952, it is shown here in milk glass.

PRIVATE PURCHASE MOLDS

In addition to the small collections from American Glass and Sinclair Glass, John and Geraldine Kemple acquired several privately owned molds. Included in the group was the Lincoln Plaque, a very interesting wall plaque dating to 1901. This piece became known as Kemple item No. 23 *Lincoln Split Rail* oval plaque.

Grace Allison in the *Tri-State Trader*, January 31, 1976, tells the story behind this acquisition: "In 1901 a gentleman made the mold for a Lincoln plaque or plate and Westmoreland made 90 pieces from this mold; no more Lincoln plaques were made over this mold until Mr. Kemple purchased it. The Kemples were watching television one evening near Lincoln's birth date and upon viewing a very pleasing picture of Abe Lincoln, Mrs. Kemple remarked that his picture would be beautiful on a piece of glass. The very next day the gentleman who had designed the Lincoln plaque, three-part mold, visited the Kemple Glass Works offering to sell his mold. Mr. Kemple purchased it for $750. The mold was so heavy, however, that it had to be reworked and over 15 lbs. of excess metal removed in order to produce a good piece of glass. The Lincoln plaque was made in milk glass, amber, blue, and a few in amethyst."

Other unique purchases included two Greentown items—the *Dolphin* (with fish finial cover), and novelty *Trunk Treasure Chest* molds. The Dolphin became known as Kemple No. 59 dish, and the Trunk Treasure Chest as Kemple No. 47 novelty box (illustrated on page 117). Greentown (earlier known as Indiana Tumbler and Goblet) made three Dolphins, each distinguishable by the rim of the dolphin's mouth. One rim was smooth, one was beaded, and the third had a sawtooth edge, resembling "teeth." The latter was Kemple's purchase. Restaurants on the East Coast used the Kemple Dolphin reproductions for serving shrimp cocktail.

The Dolphin was shown at the Pan-American Exposition in Buffalo, New York, in May 1901, by the National Glass Company's Indiana Tumbler and Goblet Works. This factory burned to the ground on June 13, 1903, and the Dolphin disappeared until Kemple purchased the mold in 1952.

Indiana Tumbler and Goblet was founded in February 1894, with David C. Jenkins, Thomas Jenkins, David Jenkins, Lewis Jenkins, and Charles Miller, Jr. as directors. Operations began on June 11, 1894. In the beginning, the firm manufactured pressed jars and containers, but soon produced full sets of glassware. Charles E. Beam succeeded Miller as Greentown's designer in 1897, responsible for most of the company's novelty wares, pitchers and the Dolphin dish.

In 1962, Joe St. Clair of St. Clair Glass in Elwood, Indiana produced another dolphin mold from the Greentown original. A mistake was made in its production, and one of the teeth was omitted from the rim, leaving nine on one side, and ten on the other. St. Clair produced dolphins in light and dark Chocolate Slag with a marking on the inside of the tail that read "Joe St. Clair." Later on, this St. Clair mold was sold to Russell Vogelsong of Summit Glass in Ohio. He also produced Dolphins in several colors.

Collectors should be aware of the differences. The Kemple Dolphin had a rim with ten teeth on each side, therefore we can say it was made from the original Greentown mold. Kemple manufactured this Dolphin in milk glass, amber, amberina, amethyst, blue, Centennial Red, cobalt, End of Day, gray, green, and teal.

Indiana Tumbler and Goblet also made covered dishes including a Hen and Rabbit, in crystal and colored glass. The Greentown Hen has a deeply scalloped tail and highly detailed feathers. The McKee Hen was less detailed. The 5¹/₂" Greentown Rabbit was made on a basketweave base, in various colors, as well as chocolate glass, a color attributed to the plant's chemist, Jacob Rosenthal.

The Kemples purchased a Hobnail master salt from owner Pete Zarilla. Collectors have since acquired this piece, Kemple No. 67, in milk glass, amber, amberina, amethyst, blue, and green.

An assortment of lamps and lamp bases in milk glass were made by Kemple Glass Works on contract, including No. 350 table lamp, No. 297 table lamp, No. 351 table lamp parts, and No. 298-99 table lamp parts.

FREE HAND

Free hand pieces were designed and manufactured by Kemple Glass employees. We have identified both the No. 239, free hand Fish ivy holder, and the No. 269 free hand Swan vase in five sizes. These were blown glass pieces, using no molds. The Fish figurine was made in milk glass, amber, amber with blue fins, blue, blue with yellow fins, and green. There was also a Fish-shaped ivy vase—the vase designed to rest on the fish's lower fins—in a crackle pattern. This piece was made in milk glass, amber, blue, and green. Kemple employees also designed two or three blown paperweights, which were sold in the gift shops.

This chapter concludes our discussion of the molds purchased over the years by the Kemple Glass Works. Some uncertainty remains as to when these molds were purchased. Efforts were made to list all known pieces, but it is entirely possible that some items were overlooked.

The Kemples were drawn to attractive or unique designs, thereby building a collection of molds that was very diverse. They acquired molds that were both popular and rare, common and uncommon. During its 25-year history, Kemple Glass made thousands of items in at least 20 different colors. Hopefully, the information presented here will assist collectors in their pursuit of this beautiful glassware.

An assortment of whimseys and miscellaneous pieces, some of them created free hand by Kemple workers. This photo appears in color on page 73.

CHAPTER SEVEN

THE WHEATON STORY

On July 1, 1970, a letter from Frank H. Wheaton, Jr., president of the Wheaton Glass Company, Millville, New Jersey, was sent to Geraldine Kemple, expressing Mr. Wheaton's surprise at learning John Kemple had passed away. Wheaton had met the Kemples some time earlier, and inquired as to whether John would consider operating a new glass plant installed in Millville as part of Wheaton Village.

He writes: "He seemed quite enthusiastic about it at the time and the purpose of my call was to see whether or not he still had the same enthusiasm and, if so, we could make some arrangement relative to the molds and his coming with the Historical Association...

"...In view of the fact that you have a great number of old molds similar to that which we would like to display, and in some cases use to manufacture in the exhibit, I am wondering if some arrangement can be made for the Historical Association to purchase these molds."

Initially, Wheaton mentioned that the Historical Association's interest was in preserving old molds to display: "We would greatly appreciate hearing from you as to whether or not the molds will be for sale and whether you would like to have them preserved in an institute like the Wheaton Historical Association." Zane Field, in *Collector's Weekly*, November 23, 1971, confirmed Wheaton Historical Association's original intent to preserve the molds, and produce glassware in some of them.

Two weeks later, on July 15, 1970, Mrs. Kemple sold 804 molds to Wheaton Industries. These included 630 press and blown molds, 48 wooden molds, 14 optic molds, 98 paste molds, and 14 blocks . (For a complete inventory of these molds, se pages 124-127.)

Gay LeCleire Taylor, curator at Wheaton Village's Museum of American Glass, said in a lecture on Kemple that "the pile of 804 molds covers an area of the warehouse 20 feet by 100 feet and 3 feet high. Press molds alone weigh over 30,000 pounds."

Ms. Taylor's lecture was devoted to the subject of these molds and the artistry behind them. Since 1975, Taylor said, Wheaton Industries had been housing them in their operating glass factory, and at a warehouse across town called the mill property.

Taylor emphasized the amount of skilled workmanship needed to create a single mold. An iron mold with a smooth interior would arrive from the foundry in the general shape of the glass piece. Lathes, files and chisels were used to carve the design into the mold. This process could take from 87 to 378 hours per mold, depending on the complexity of the design. The molds were, in themselves, small masterpieces.

This storage area held up to 1,100 molds by the time John E. Kemple Glass Works was sold. Wheaton Industries purchased 804 of them, covering an area of their warehouse 20 feet by 100 feet.

A color flyer, advertising *Wheatonware Hand-Pressed Kemple Reproductions*.
This assortment was offered in amber and blue.

Some molds were created in one piece, others in two or three pieces. The intricately carved *Wiltec Shamrock* dish (Kemple No. 103), and the split rib base to the 5½" covered animal dishes are examples of one-piece molds.

Antique molds have two "enemies" of which Ms. Taylor spoke. First, the World War I and World War II metal drives caused all available iron material to be scrapped for tanks, guns, and ships. Second, the open air in most storage areas emits oxides that can rust cast iron molds. Humidity damages them as well, and cold weather allows parts on the molds to freeze or lock, causing the designs to split. Molds in long-term storage were usually protected with a coat of oil, but even the oil collected dust, making them dirty and more difficult to use.

Soon after Wheaton Industries acquired the Kemple molds, they began to make items for their Wheatonware division. At first, there were no distinguishing marks other than the original "K". At Mrs. Kemple's request, however, a small "w" was carved into the molds near the "K," so that Wheaton's reproductions could be distinguished from Kemple's.

WHEATONWARE

Wheatonware was established in 1965, as a division of the Wheaton Glass Company. It operated like Tupperware, and Mary Kay, with sales representatives conducting home parties. From 1970-1975, representatives added Kemple pieces to their lines, traveling from home to home with glass tableware in popular patterns such as *Moon & Star Variant*, and *Yutec*. At its height, the company had over 2,000 independent contractors or representatives, conducting home parties.

Colorful flyers were printed, advertising *Wheatonware Hand-Pressed Kemple Reproductions*, Kemple patterns that became marketable lines for home sales and tableware parties. These flyers illustrated the following pieces in blue and amber: three *Belles*, *Dutch Boy and Girl*, *Mary* and *Christ* plate, *Mary* and *Christ* plaques, *Haley's* compote, *Napoleon's* hat, *Dolphin* dish, *Moon & Star Variant* dishes, *Clover-Leaf* ash tray, assortment of "Tec" patterns in bowls, covered butter, and plates; *Lace and Dewdrop* goblets, pitcher and glasses, compote, bowls, and plates; *Sawtooth* candlesticks.

The flyers also illustrated—in green—tableware in *Moon & Star Variant*, and *Prescut* patterns.

In 1975, the I.R.S. took Wheatonware to court (in addition to two other small firms) to require them to make Social Security payments for their sales agents. Frank Wheaton decided to close the division, as it was only marginally profitable. The suit was settled out of court one year later. Ironically, the I.R.S. lost its case, and now, companies are only required to issue a 1099 form to their sales people.

In 1975, the Kemple molds were transferred to the Wheaton Historical Association, (reorganized as the Wheaton Cultural Alliance, Inc.) the governing body of Wheaton Village. Though later that year some molds would be removed for production of the Wheatoncraft line, many of them remain there in storage at the time of this writing.

Color flyer advertising Wheatonware. This Lace and Dewdrop assortment was offered in amber and blue.

This flyer displays an amber, blue and green assortment of Wheatonware, consisting of the following Kemple items: the Moon & Star Variant bowl; Narcissus candlesticks; Prescut open compote, sugars, creamers, and covered butter; and Sawtooth candlesticks.

Portions of a December 1974 price list for Wheatonware, a division of Wheaton Industries, which made and sold Kemple reproductions. This price list was made available to each person attending a home party put on by Wheatonware's sales representatives. The item numbers shown are Wheatonware's, not to be confused with Kemple product numbers.

KEMPLE COLLECTORS ITEMS
SUBJECT TO AVAILABILITY

Item	Description	Price	
150A	Old Boston Candy Dish Amber	13.95	
150B	Old Boston Candy Dish Blue	13.95	
152A	Antique Mint Dish Amber	7.50	
152B	Antique Mint Dish Blue	7.50	
152G	Antique Mint Dish Green	7.50	
154A	Early American Fruit Bowl Amber	16.50	
154B	Early American Fruit Bowl Blue	16.50	
154G	Early American Fruit Bowl Green	16.50	
156A★	Combination Special of No. 152 and No. 154 Amber (Save 4.05)	19.95	
156B★	Combination Special of No. 152 and No. 154 Blue (Save 4.05)	19.95	
156G★	Combination Special of No. 152 and No. 154 Green (Save 4.05)	19.95	
158A	Dolphin Condiment Jar with Glass Spoon Amber	14.50	
158B	Dolphin Condiment Jar with Glass Spoon Blue	14.50	
158G	Dolphin Condiment Jar with Glass Spoon Green	14.50	
159A	Glass Spoon Amber	2.95	
159B	Glass Spoon Blue	2.95	
159G	Glass Spoon Green	2.95	
160A	Southern Belle Figurine Amber	4.95	
160B	Southern Belle Figurine Blue	4.95	
160P	Southern Belle Figurine Oriental Pearl Crystal	5.25	
162A	Colonial Lady Figurine Amber	4.95	
162B	Colonial Lady Figurine Blue	4.95	
162P	Colonial Lady Figurine - Oriental Pearl Crystal	5.25	
164A	Victorian Lady Figurine Amber	4.95	
164B	Victorian Lady Figurine Blue	4.95	
164P	Victorian Lady Figurine - Oriental Pearl Crystal	5.25	
166A★	Set of 3 Above 160, 162, 164 Amber (Save 1.00)	13.85	
166B★	Set of 3 Above 160, 162, 164 Blue (Save 1.00)	13.85	
166P★	Set of 3 Above 160, 162, 164 Oriental Pearl Crystal (Save 1.00)	14.75	
168	Boy Girl Bookends Blue	7.95	
170A	Free Form Ashtray Amber	14.50	
170B	Free Form Ashtray Blue	14.50	
172A	Cranberry Bowl Amber	8.50	
172B	Cranberry Bowl Blue	8.50	
174A	Clover Dish Amber	6.75	
174B	Clover Dish Blue	6.75	
176A	Spoon Holder Amber	6.95	
176B	Spoon Holder Blue	6.95	
178A	Glass Lace Plate (6'') Amber	4.25	
178B	Glass Lace Plate (6'') Blue	4.25	
180A	Glass Lace Plate (7½'') Amber	4.75	
180B	Glass Lace Plate (7½'') Blue	4.75	
182A	Glass Lace Plate (9'') Amber	5.25	
182B	Glass Lace Plate (9'') Blue	5.25	
183A	Glass Lace Plates - Set of 3 Amber (Save 1.30	12.95	
	TOTAL COLUMN ONE		

KEMPLE COLLECTORS ITEMS
SUBJECT TO AVAILABILITY

Item	Description	Price	
183B	Glass Lace Plates - Set of 3 Blue (Save 1.30)	12.95	
184A	Pedestal Compote Amber	16.95	
184B	Pedestal Compote Blue	16.95	
184G	Pedestal Compote Green	16.95	
186A	Glass Boat Server Amber	7.95	
186B	Glass Boat Server Blue	7.95	
188A	Glass Wall Plaque-Madonna Amber	3.75	
188B	Glass Wall Plaque-Madonna Blue	3.75	
190A	Glass Wall Plaque-Jesus Amber	3.75	
190B	Glass Wall Plaque-Jesus Blue	3.75	
192A★	Wall Plaque Set: Madonna-Jesus Amber (Save 1.50)	6.00	
192B★	Wall Plaque Set: Madonna-Jesus Blue (Save 1.50)	6.00	
194A	Bon Bon Dish with Glass Loop Handle Amber	8.50	
194B	Bon Bon Dish with Glass Loop Handle Blue	8.50	
196A	Covered Round Butter Dish Amber	14.50	
196B	Covered Round Butter Dish Blue	14.50	
196G	Covered Round Butter Dish Green	14.50	
198A	Moon-Star Thumbprint Compote Amber	14.50	
198B	Moon-Star Thumbprint Compote Blue	14.50	
198G	Moon-Star Thumbprint Compote Green	14.50	
198P	Moon-Star Thumbprint Compote Oriental Pearl Crystal	15.50	
200A	Footed Wed'g Comp. w/lid Amber	13.95	
200B	Footed Wed'g Comp. w/lid Blue	13.95	
200G	Footed Wed'g Comp. w/lid Green	13.95	
200P	Footed Wed'g Comp. w/lid- Oriental Pearl Crystal	14.50	
202A	Midnight Star Serving Tray Amber	10.95	
202B	Midnight Star Serving Tray Blue	10.95	
204A	Cream Pitcher Amber	7.50	
204B	Cream Pitcher Blue	7.50	
206A	Candy & Sugar Bowl Amber	11.95	
206B	Candy & Sugar Bowl Blue	11.95	
208A★	Combination of #202, 204, 206 Total Value 29.25 (Save 4.45) Amber	25.95	
208B★	Combination of #202, 204, 206 Total Value 29.25 (Save 4.45) Blue	25.95	
210A	Traditional Glass Loop Candle Holders Amber (Pair)	12.50	
210B	Traditional Glass Loop Candle Holders Blue (Pair)	12.50	
212A	Pedestal Bowl Candle Holders Amber (Pair)	12.50	
212B	Pedestal Bowl Candle Holders Blue (Pair)	12.50	
212G	Pedestal Bowl Candle Holders Green (Pair)	12.50	
214A	Rolled Floral Leaf Candle Holders Amber (Pair)	12.50	

DECORAMA GUIDE

ITEM NUMBER	DESCRIPTION	TOTAL QUAN.	PRICE	TOTAL
	KEMPLE COLLECTORS ITEMS **SUBJECT TO AVAILABILITY**			
214B	Rolled Floral Leaf Candle Holders Blue (Pair)		12.50	
216A	Saw-Tooth Candle Holders Amber (Pair)		12.50	
216B	Saw-Tooth Candle Holders Blue (Pair)		12.50	
218A	Lilly Pad Candle Holders Amber (Pair)		12.50	
218B	Lilly Pad Candle Holders Blue (Pair)		12.50	

ITEM NUMBER	DESCRIPTION	TOTAL QUAN.	PRICE	TOTAL
	KEMPLE DINNERWARE EACH PIECE HANDPRESSED	**LACE AND DEWDROP PATTERN**		
250A	10'' Plate Amber		8.50	
250B	10'' Plate Blue		8.50	
250G	10'' Plate Green		8.50	
252A	8'' Plate Amber		7.00	
252B	8'' Plate Blue		7.00	
252G	8'' Plate Green		7.00	
254A	Cup & Saucer Amber		7.50	
254B	Cup & Saucer Blue		7.50	
254G	Cup & Saucer Green		7.50	
256A	Saucer Only Amber		4.00	
256B	Saucer Only Blue		4.00	
256G	Saucer Only Green		4.00	
258A	Footed Soup Cup Amber		4.90	
258B	Footed Soup Cup Blue		4.90	
258G	Footed Soup Cup Green		4.90	
260A★	5 pc. Plate Setting (Save 1.40) incl #250, 252, 254, 258 Amber		26.50	
260B★	5 pc. Place Setting (Save 1.40) incl #250, 252, 254, 258 Blue		26.50	
260G★	5 pc. Place Setting (Save 1.40) incl #250, 252, 254, 258 Green		26.50	
262A★	3 pc. Starter Set (Save 1.00) incl #250, 254 Amber		15.00	
262B★	3 pc. Starter Set (Save 1.00) incl #250, 254 Blue		15.00	
262G★	3 pc. Starter Set (Save 1.00) incl. #250, 254 Green		15.00	
268A	Tumbler - 6 oz. Amber		6.00	
268B	Tumbler - 6 oz. Blue		6.00	
268G	Tumbler - 6 oz. Green		6.00	
270A★	Tumblers (Pair) Amber (Save 1.00)		11.00	
270B★	Tumblers (Pair) Blue (Save 1.00)		11.00	
270G★	Tumblers (Pair) Green (Save 1.00)		11.00	
272A	Goblet - 6 oz. Amber		7.50	
272B	Goblet - 6 oz. Blue		7.50	
272G	Goblet - 6 oz. Green		7.50	
274A★	Goblets (Pair) Amber (Save 1.00)		14.00	
274B★	Goblets (Pair) Blue (Save 1.00)		14.00	
274G★	Goblets (Pair) Green (Save 1.00)		14.00	
276A	Pitcher - 25 oz. Amber		14.00	
276B	Pitcher - 25 oz. Blue		14.00	
276G	Pitcher - 25 oz. Green		14.00	
278A	Sugar & Creamer Amber		10.95	
278B	Sugar & Creamer Blue		10.95	
278G	Sugar & Creamer Green		10.95	
280A	Covered Butter Dish Amber		11.95	
280B	Covered Butter Dish Blue		11.95	

ITEM NUMBER	**KEMPLE DINNERWARE** EACH PIECE HANDPRESSED	**LACE AND DEWDROP PATTERN**	PRICE	TOTAL
280G	Covered Butter Dish Green		11.95	
262A	10'' Serving Bowl Amber		9.95	
282B	10'' Serving Bowl Blue		9.95	
282G	10'' Serving Bowl Green		9.95	
284A	8'' Serv'g Bowl w/cover Amber		13.95	
284B	8'' Serv'g Bowl w/cover Blue		13.95	
284G	8'' Serv'g Bowl w/cover Green		13.95	
286A	6'' Serv'g Bowl w/cover Amber		9.95	
286B	6'' Serv'g Bowl w/cover Blue		9.95	
286G	6'' Serv'g Bowl w/cover Green		9.95	
288A	4'' Serving Bowl Amber		5.50	
288B	4'' Serving Bowl Blue		5.50	
288G	4'' Serving Bowl Green		5.50	
290A	Candle Holders Amber		10.50	
290B	Candle Holders Blue		10.50	
290G	Candle Holders Green		10.50	
292A	Free Form Vase Amber		12.50	
292B	Free Form Vase Blue		12.50	
292G	Free Form Vase Green		12.50	
294A★	Set of Bowls (4 #288) Total Value 22.00 (Save 5.50) Amber		16.50	
294B★	Set of Bowls (4 #288) Total Value 22.00 (Save 5.50) Blue		16.50	
294G★	Set of Bowls (4 #288) Total Value 22.00 (Save 5.50) Green		16.50	

ITEM NUMBER	**KEMPLE MINIATURES** **SUBJECT TO AVAILABILITY**		PRICE	TOTAL
746A	Cherub Lighter (Amber with Gold Lighter)		7.50	
746B	Cherub Lighter (Blue with Silver Lighter)		7.50	
748A ★	Cherub Lighter & Cherub Cup Cigarette Jar-Set (Save 95¢)		11.50	
748B ★	Cherub Lighter & Cherub Cup Cigarette Jar-Set (Save 95¢)		11.50	
750A	Cherub Cup Amber		4.95	
750B	Cherub Cup Blue		4.95	
750G	Cherub Cup Green		4.95	
752A	Puss N'Boots Glass Slipper Amber		4.95	
752B	Puss N'Boots Glass Slipper Blue		4.95	
752G	Puss N'Boots Glass Slipper Green		4.95	
752P	Puss N'Boots Glass Slipper Oriental Pearl Crystal		4.95	
754A	Steamship Trunk Amber		6.95	
754B	Steamship Trunk Blue		6.95	
754G	Steamship Trunk Green		6.95	
756A	Cabbage Rose Dresser Tray w/lid Amber		6.95	
756B	Cabbage Rose Dresserb Tray w/lid Blue		6.95	
756G	Cabbage Rose Dresser Tray w/lid Green		6.95	
758A	Lion's Head Dresser Tray w/lid Amber		6.95	
758B	Lion's Head Dresser Tray w/lid Blue		6.95	
758G	Lion's Head Dresser Tray w/lid Green		6.95	
760A	Oval Dresser Tray w/lid Amber		6.95	
760B	Oval Dresser Tray w/lid Blue		6.95	
760G	Oval Dresser Tray w/lid Green		6.95	
762A	Palette Shaped Dresser Tray w/lid Amber		6.95	
762B	Palette Shaped Dresser Tray w/lid Blue		6.95	

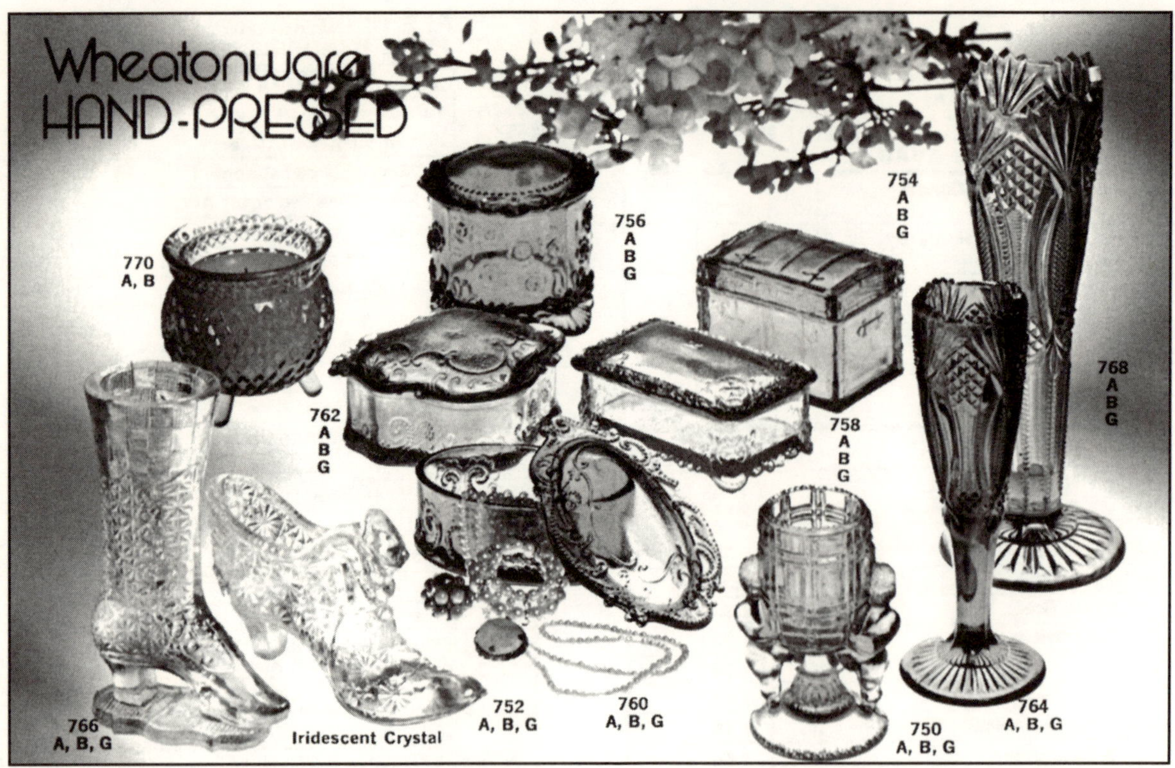

A colored flyer from Wheatonware's Treasure Envelopes. This flyer advertises Wheatonware hand-pressed reproductions. Shown in this flyer are the Gypsy Kettle toothpick, marketed here as a votive candleholder; Daisy & Button boot vase and Puss-in-Boot slipper; Beaded Scroll dresser boxes; Trunk treasure chest; Cherub cup; and Jubilee tall celery or vase.

WHEATONCRAFT

Wheatoncraft was established in late 1975, as another division of the Wheaton Glass Company. Unlike Wheatonware, this product line was not available through home parties, catalogs, or mail order flyers. It was available in retail stores and the Wheaton Village Gift Shop. Like Wheatonware, the Wheatoncraft line included other types of glass, mostly with a Bicentennial theme, in addition to its featured Kemple pieces.

Wheatoncraft was originally the name of Wheaton Industries' old hand shop, hence their logo: "Creators of Hand Made Glassware." Both the Wheatonware and Wheatoncraft lines were hand-pressed, and manufactured without using automated machinery.

These products were pressed and sold until 1979, when the molds were discontinued and returned to storage. Wheaton Industries has not manufactured any Kemple reproductions since that time.

KEMPLE MOLDS

Wheaton Industries created an inventory of all the molds purchased from Mrs. Kemple, dated July 15, 1970. The following is a comprehensive list. Wherever possible, we have tried to use descriptions the company used when taking inventory of these molds.

Over 100 **Mannington** molds were included in Wheaton's purchases. Grouped by pattern name or type, they were:

Beaded Scroll: dresser box with cover, pen box with cover

Beaded Swirl: 7" pin tray

Cabbage Rose: two different trays, dresser jar with cover, jewel box with cover, mug, 9" plate

Fleur-de-Lis: 7" Lace Edge plate, 6" Lace Edge plate, soap dish with cover, powder jar with cover

Lacy Heart: two 6" plates

Novelties: Waffle Hat toothpick, Indian Head toothpick, 3-handled Pansy toothpick, Indian Chief match holder, Basket Weave basket, Large Lion Head tray, Horse Shoe Tray, Heart-shaped tray, Shell-shaped tray, five different trays, Spade-Heart-Club-Diamond ash trays, three different ash trays, 5½" Christ & Mary plaques, Cupid plaque, Angel plaque, Coal Bucket, Narcissus candle holder, Daisy & Button 6" boot vase, Daisy

& Button "Puss in Boot" slipper, Lion Head rectangular dresser box with cover, Lion Head round dresser box with cover, novelty box with cover, and 6", 7", and 8¹/₂" Sheaf of Wheat plate

Scroll with Fleur-de-Lis: powder jar with cover

Scroll with Flower: dresser box with cover, hanky box with cover, and pomade with cover

Versailles: dresser box with cover, oblong dresser box with cover, and cigarette box with cover

Plates: Lovers' Knot 8¹/₂" Lace Edge, Shell & Club 7" and 9¹/₂" Lace Edge, Maple Leaf 8" Open Edge, Inverted Heart 7" Open Edge, Mary & Christ, Angel Head 8¹/₂" Open Edge, and a 9" 101-Lace Edge

Unidentified: three puff boxes with covers, large cigarette box with cover, toothpick or jar, glove box with cover, and 3¹/₂" tiny novelty tray.

At least 82 of the **Tuska** molds were included in Wheaton's purchases. Grouped by pattern name, they were:

Blackberry: 5" and 8" bowl, 4¹/₂" and 6" candlestick, 7" candlestick, creamer, sugar, 5" candy with cover, goblet, 4", 5", 6", and 7" nappy

Ivy-in-Snow: 10" dinner plate, 7" lunch plate, 8" dish, 8" cover, 7" cover, 8" nappy, 7" nappy, 6" bowl, bowl/nappy, jelly, deep tray or banana split dish, pickle dish, sugar with cover, creamer, butter cover, cup, saucer, 3 pint water pitcher, claret, goblet, wine, tumbler, ice tea mug, candlestick, footed celery vase, and tall celery

Lace & Dewdrop: 10" bowl with cover, 8" bowl with cover, 6" bowl with cover, Top Hat vase/bowl, sugar bowl with cover, creamer, small creamer, small sugar, 4" nappy, butter with cover, wedding jar or compote with cover, sherbet, 7" plate, 10" plate, large candle holder, small candle holder, 8" tall footed celery, tumbler, 36 oz. water pitcher, cup, and a goblet

Moon & Star Variant: 3-toe candle holder, bowl with foot, and 8" bowl

Sawtooth: candle holder.

Over 300 of the **McKee** molds were included in Wheaton's purchases. Grouped by pattern name, they were:

Official letterhead logo from Wheaton Village, a division of Wheaton Cultural Alliance, Inc.

Aztec: 8¹/₂" vase, 8" compote, 2-handled compote, 5¹/₂" handled bon bon, goblet, and bottle

Banzantine: 2-handled toothpick, footed sugar, footed creamer, candle holder, mustard dish with cover, two shells, salt, Loving Cup, and vase

Bontec: 6" 3-toe bon bon, footed sherbet, footed toothpick, footed nut cup, tumbler, ice tea, ice tub, and pickle tray

Carltec: 2-handled compote, 4 oz. claret, square sugar, and square creamer

Covered Animal Dishes: Fox 7¹/₂" top, Rooster 7¹/₂" top, Hen 7¹/₂" top, Cow 7¹/₂" top, Lion 7¹/₂" top, Basket Weave 7¹/₂" nest, Horse 5¹/₂" top, Turkey 5¹/₂" top, Cat 5¹/₂" top, Duck 5¹/₂" top, Dove 5¹/₂" top, Rooster 5¹/₂" top, Hen 5¹/₂" top, Lamb 5¹/₂" top, Rabbit 5¹/₂" top, and Split Rib 5¹/₂" nest

Innovation: Napoleon's Hat (Cane Band & Rose design)

Lacey Heart: bottle

Martec: 7" triangular tidbit tray, pickle or olive tray, long pickle tray, 7" 2-handled bon bon, 3-toe bon bon, bon bon with handle, 7" wine, small wine, 13" canoe, bud vase, compote, jelly compote, claret, long basket, 10" fruit bowl, and oblong bowl

Natural Crackle: bottle

Novelty Items: Lincoln Hat toothpick, Cherub toothpick, 3-toe Gypsy Kettle toothpick, 3-toe Gypsy Kettle ash tray, Helping Hand ash tray, Square Wedding Jar 6" footed candy with cover, Hobstar & Fan candy with cover, Art Dressed vase, Diamond salt dip, Horse Shoe pen rack, and Westward Ho goblet

Pineapple: tall stem jelly compote, and sherbet

Wheaton Glass Company's logo, as taken from the letterhead on which Frank H. Wheaton, Jr. wrote to Mrs. Kemple on July 1, 1970 requesting purchase of the Kemple molds.

Plain/Optic: two cruets, pinched ewer, four bottles, Panel ewer, three large bottle stoppers, bulbous pitcher, butter with cover, compote with cover, toast mug, sugar or cream, medium ash tray, candle holder, and tall vase

Plutec: 4" nappy, and compote

Plytec: 3", 5", and 7" bowl

Puritan: whiskey

Rainbow: bottle, and wine

Ribbed: bottle, and 4-toe salt dip

Rotec: 4" nappy, $4^{1}/_{2}$" nappy, butter with cover, large sugar, large creamer, 8" bowl, and bottle

Sandwich: two different goblets, two different cocktails, two juice cups, ice tea, tall footed candy with cover, sherbet, dessert, sugar, and creamer

Sextec: 3 pint pitcher, 2-handled sugar, creamer, butter with cover, salt and pepper, spoon holder, and jelly compote

Sunburst: 6" tall bud vase, $8^{1}/_{2}$" tall vase, cruet, petticoat cruet, and 6" bowl

Swirl: bottle

Toltec: $6^{1}/_{2}$" bowl, 6" nappy, two different creamers, sugar, handled bon bon, footed jelly compote, goblet, and bottle

Waffle & Button: miniature sugar with cover, miniature butter with cover, miniature creamer, and miniature toothpick

Wiltec: $8^{1}/_{2}$" vase, footed jelly compote, shamrock and olive tray

Yutec: $8^{1}/_{2}$" tray, celery tray, candy jar or old sugar, cover for candy jar or old sugar, two different sugars with cover, creamer with cover, open sugar or spoon holder, 13 oz. creamer, creamer, compote, two different butters with cover, salt dip, celery vase or spoon holder, spoon or open sugar, two salt and peppers, toothpick, cranberry bowl, 10" bowl, 8" bowl, $4^{1}/_{2}$" nappy, 6" pickle dish, 6" nappy foot, 3 pint water pitcher, decanter, cruet, tumbler cordial, tall stem chalice, punch bowl, foot for punch bowl, goblet, cocktail, champagne, wine, whiskey, candle holder, and $8^{1}/_{2}$" vase.

The **Sinclair** molds include the *Square Lace Edge* cup, Square Lace Edge saucer, Square 8" Lace Edge plate, *Rib Base* cigarette box bottom with ash tray top, ash tray with lighter holder, 6" ash tray and match holder.

The **American Glass Co.** molds were represented by the *Indian Head* ash tray, *Horse Head* ash tray, *Cleopatra* and *Caesar* ash trays, *Hob Nail* ash tray, *Fighting Cock* bookend, *Dutch Boy* and *Dutch Girl* bookends, *Horse* figurine/bookends, *Bird of Paradise* figurine, *Female Pheasant* figurine, *Male Pheasant* figurine, *Southern Belle* figurine, *Victorian Lady* figurine, *Colonial Lady* figurine, *Deer (Llama)* figurine, *Pony & Cart* toothpick, *Stage Coach* box with cover, *Church Lamp* top, Church Lamp bottom, and *Haley's compote.*

The **private purchase** molds included the *Hobnail* 3-toe candle holder or toothpick, Hobnail master salt tub, Hobnail bowl, *Dolphin* bottom with Fish cover, *Trunk Treasure Chest,* and Split Rail *Lincoln* plaque.

The **free hand,** or free-blown, molds included two different lamp bases, two different lamp blow molds, five lamp molds, 14 blow molds for making eggs, seven molds for paperweights, decanter, oil bottle, and the Star-shaped paperweight or ash tray.

Finally, there were some **"unidentified"** molds included in the purchase: two different cookie jars, two different photo holders, two different napkin holders, spoon holder, two small boats, two plain molds, salt dip, small salt dip, 10" oblong 4-toe orange bowl, 10" bowl, 8" 3-toe bowl, 6" tray, 17 different trays, star-shaped tray, heart-shaped tray, 9" plate, 8" plate, 7" plate, 6" plate, bon bon box, box with cover, square jar, hatchet, 8" square candle holder, candleholder, footed wine or toothpick, compote, mug, vase, three different bottles, and a mold for making three stoppers at once.

CONCLUSION

This chapter on the Wheaton purchase brings to a close our story of John and Geraldine Kemple and the John E. Kemple Glass Works. It began with a "chance meeting on a bus" during the early years of World War II and ended with John's passing in 1970. Though Kemple Glass Works was never very large nor well-renown, its story and its products are part of the American glass heritage. Its legacy to the world of glass collectors was high quality milk and colored glass reproductions of some very unique patterns.

Unlike many other factories who made their own molds or gradually developed successful lines of glass by trial and error, Kemple Glass existed by purchasing batches of old, retired molds from various factories and resurrecting them. For several decades, they were able to make beautiful pattern glass reproductions from these "antique" molds. Combined with John's glassmaking experience and Geraldine's business sense, the purchased molds became the basis for Kemple Glass Works' existence and profitability.

As has been true since the beginning of pattern glass production, retired molds still in existence remain valuable as potential producers of glass. The Kemple molds—created elsewhere and purchased to make their company successful—now reside at Wheaton Village. While the Kemple Glass Works is now a part of history, who knows where these molds will resurface again? Perhaps they will remain at Wheaton Village forever; and perhaps not.

Advertising art used in early promotional material for
the gas-heated furnace operation of glassware.

APPENDIX
CATALOG PAGE REPRINTS

No. 1—5½" Hen Covered Dish
$14.40 per Dozen

No. 20—5½" Turkey Covered Dish
$14.40 per Dozen

No. 4—5½" Rooster Covered Dish
$14.40 per Dozen

No. 15—7¼" Fox Covered Dish
$30.00 per Dozen

No. 9—5½" Lamb Covered Dish
$14.40 per Dozen

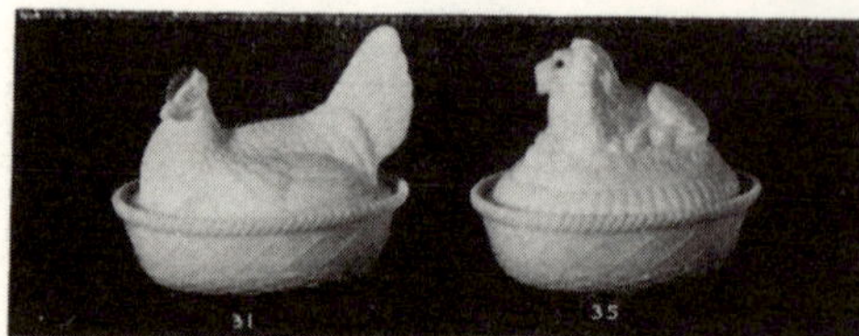

No. 31—7¼" Hen Covered Dish
$21.60 per Dozen

No. 35—7¼" Lion Covered Dish
$24.00 per Dozen

No. 25—5½" Cat Covered Dish
$14.40 per Dozen

No. 26—5½" Rabbit Covered Dish
$14.40 per Dozen

No. 36—5½" Horse Covered Dish
$14.40 per Dozen

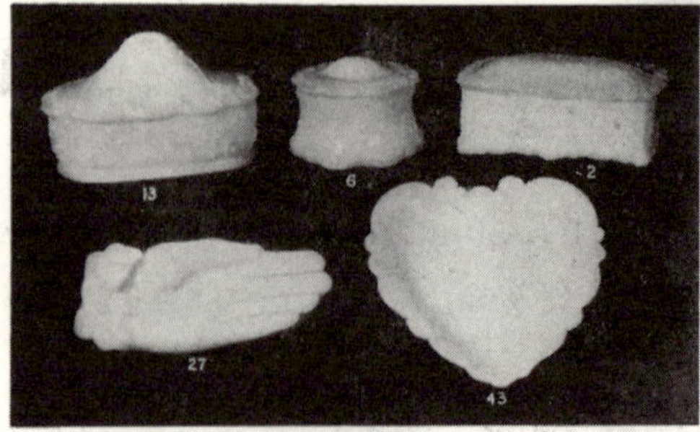

No. 13—Novelty Box
$13.20 per Dozen

No. 6—Pomade Box
$8.40 per Dozen

No. 2—Novelty Box
$13.20 per Dozen

No. 27—Hand Ash Tray or Spoon Rest
$6.00 per Dozen

No. 43—4½" by 4½" Heart Shaped Tray
$7.20 per Dozen

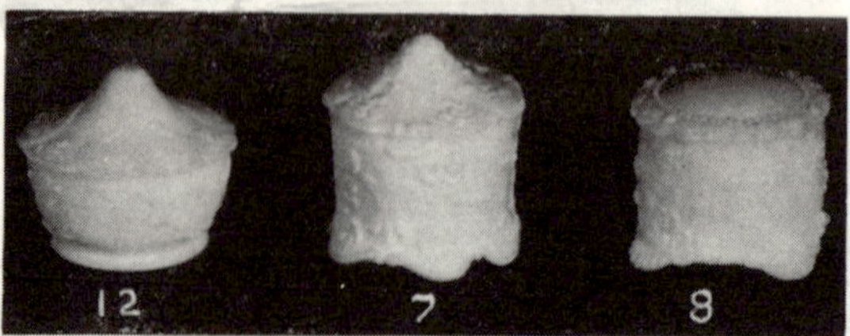

No. 12—Powder Box
$13.20 per Dozen

No. 7—Puff Box
$14.40 per Dozen

No. 8—Puff Box
$14.40 per Dozen

No. 28—5½" Dove Covered Dish
$14.40 per Dozen

No. 33—7¼" Cow Covered Dish
$24.00 per Dozen

No. 34—5½" Bobbed Tail Duck Covered Dish
$14.40 per Dozen

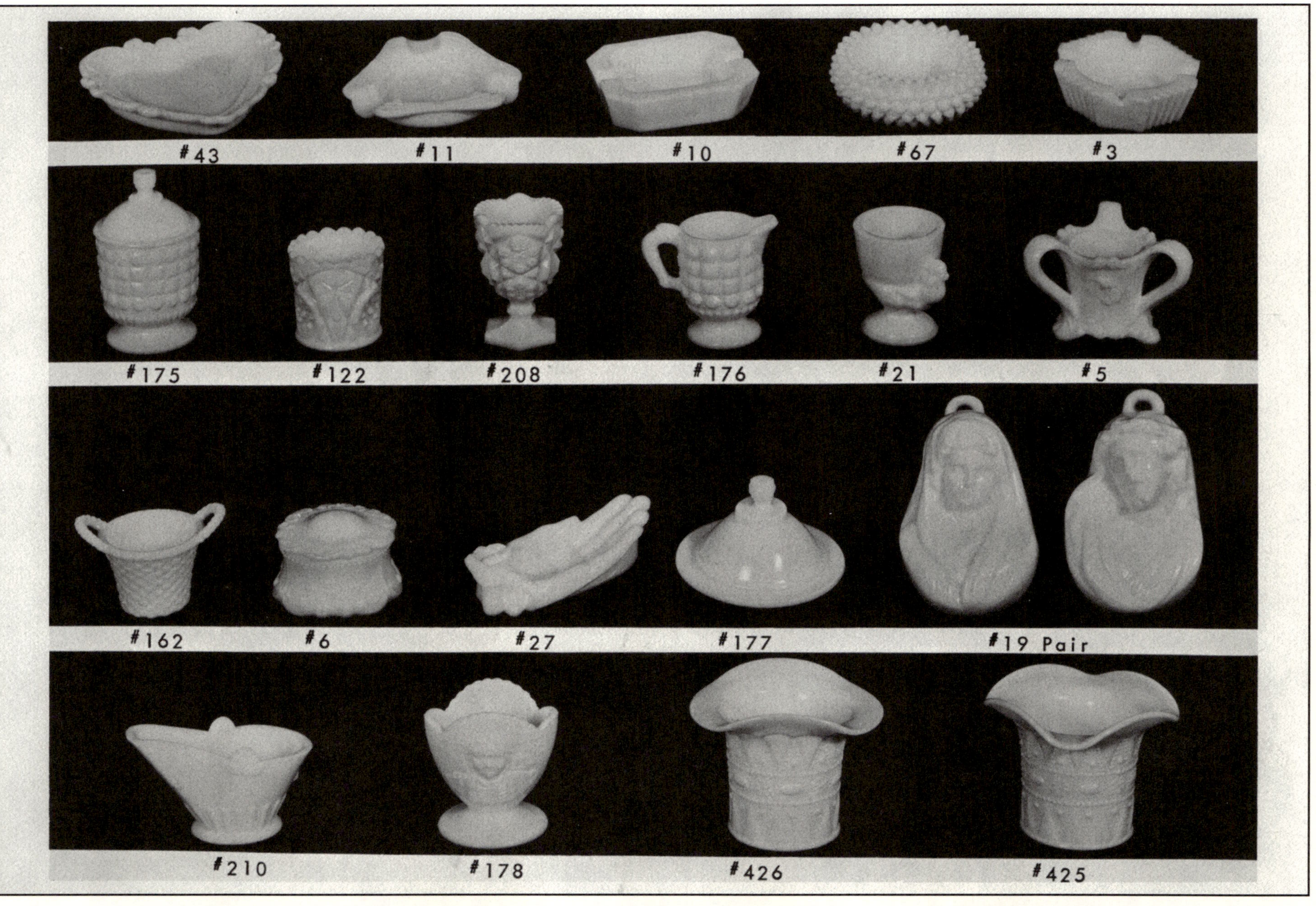

This catalog page displays an assortment of milk glass novelty items. Kemple item numbers are shown for each piece, and they can be identified according to the Item Number Index, beginning on page 137.

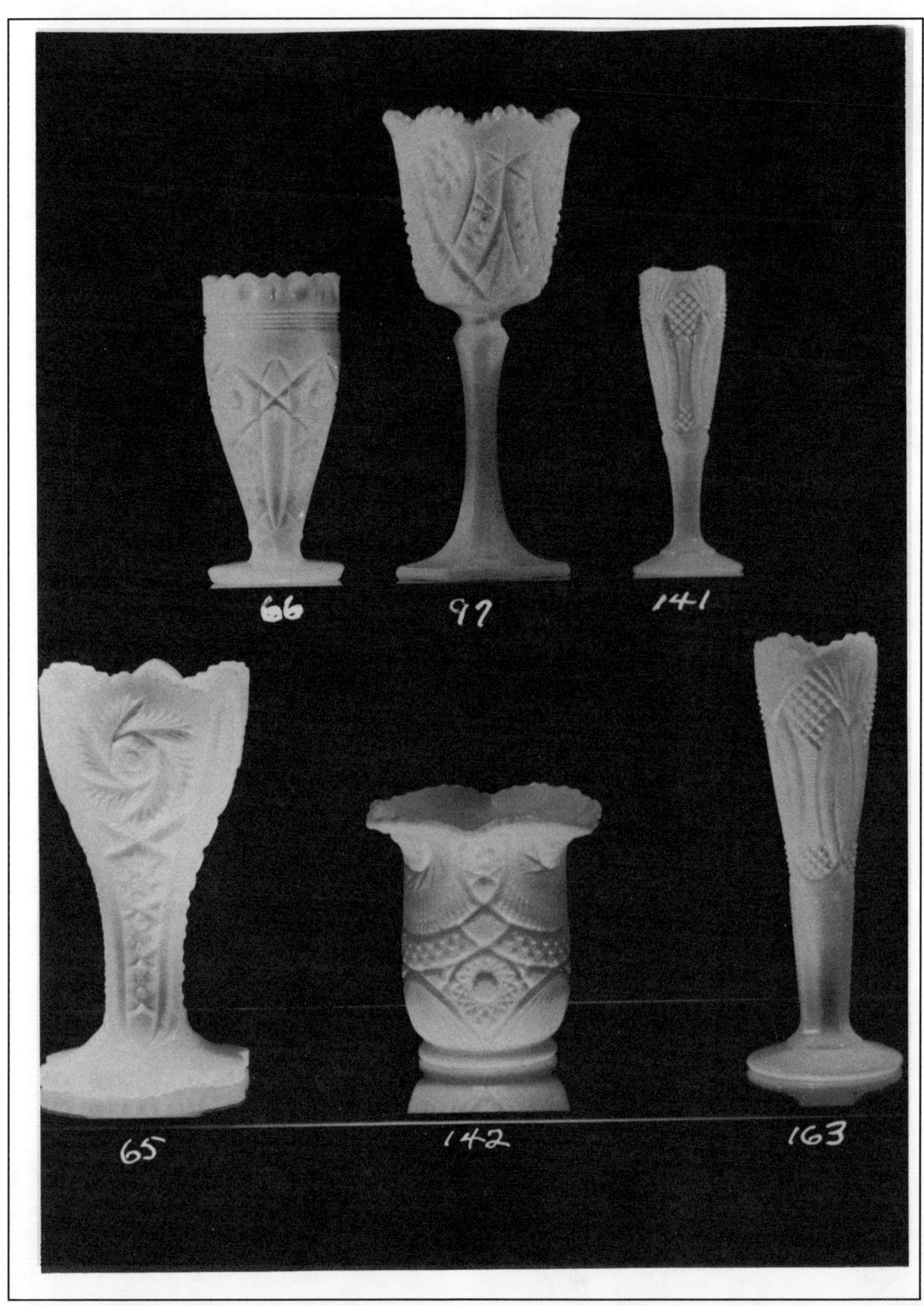

Kemple catalog page displaying milk glass. *Top row*: No. 66 Quintec footed vase, no. 97 Yutec chalice, No. 141 Jubilee 6" vase; *Bottom row:* No. 65 Wiltec footed vase, No. 142 Sunburst crimped vase, No. 163 Jubilee 8" vase.

Catalog page of milk glass items in Toltec. *Top row:* No. 207 or No. 222 whiskey or toothpick, No. 71 oval footed nut bowl, No. 213 2-handled sugar, No. 214 creamer; *Second row:* No. 216 handled 6" bon bon, No. 215 tall creamer; *Bottom row:* No. 203 bowl 6", No. 81 footed jelly.

OTHER KEMPLE ITEMS OF INTEREST

The items illustrated below are included in the Item Number index on pp. 137-150 of this book, but are not pictured elsewhere in this book, due to lack of adequate information or substantial photographs. They are illustrated here so that the reader may view the pattern in as much detail as possible.

No. 105 Innovation—Sparkle 8" bowl

No. 169 Champion condiment holder and No. 552 Champion Petticoat set of three bottles and toothpick

No. 171 Diamond Ice Tea pitcher

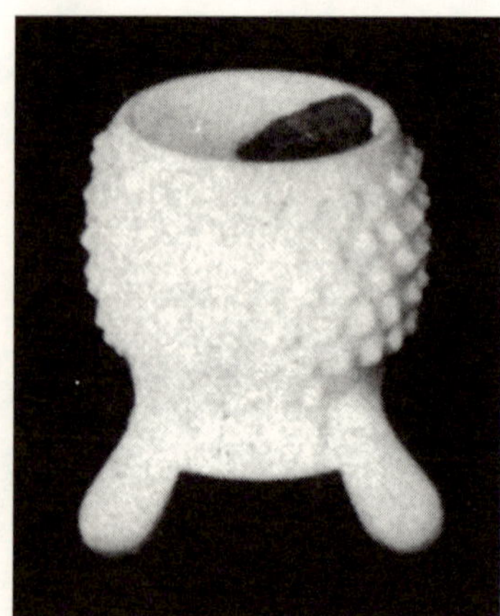

No. 76 Hobnail 3-footed candlestick

No. 157 Beaded Scroll oval dresser box with cover

This Wheatoncraft color flyer displays Kemple reproductions in crystal, identified by Wheatoncraft item number. *Clockwise from the top left their corresponding Kemple item numbers include:* No. 87 Cane Band & Rose Napoleon's Hat bowl; No. 86-A Cane Band & Rose compote base; No. 86 (both) Cane Band & Rose Napoleon's Hat on compote base; No. 70 Toltec oval footed candlesticks; No. 40 Sawtooth candlesticks; No. 311 Moon & Star Variant 11" compote; No. 94 Narcissus candlesticks; No. 141 Jubilee 6" vase; and No. 163 Jubilee 8" vase.

This flyer also displays Kemple reproductions in crystal, listed by Wheatoncraft item number. *Clockwise from the top left their corresponding Kemple item numbers include:* No. 133 Yutec covered sugar, No. 139 Yutec spooner, No. 49 Hobstar & Fan covered footed candy, No. 243 Gypsy Kettle toothpick, No. 122 Yutec toothpick, No. 119 Yutec 7" relish, No. 103 Wiltec Shamrock olive tray, No. 134 Yutec condiment tray, No. 943 Mary & Child 6" plate, No. 266 Diamond Shell spoon, No. 59 Dolphin dish, No. 106 oblong 10" bowl, and No. 140 Yutec creamer.

This color Wheatoncraft flyer displays reproductions of the Kemple 5½" covered animal dishes, on split-rib base. They are illustrated in crystal and amber, and identified by Wheatoncraft item number. *From top to bottom, their corresponding Kemple item numbers include:* No. 20 Turkey on Nest, No. 1 Hen on Nest, No. 9 Lamb on Nest, No. 4 Rooster on Nest, No. 25 Cat on Nest, and No. 36 Horse on Nest.

135

INDEXES
ITEM NUMBER INDEX
PATTERN NAME INDEX
VALUE GUIDE

☆ Hand Made Milk Glass by Kemple ☆

All Decorations Fired for Permanency

No. 54-V—Candle Holder, Violet Design
$36.00 per Dozen

No. 53-V—Planter Center Piece, Violet Design
$36.00 per Dozen

No. 55-I—Sugar and Creamer, Ivy Design
$36.00 per Dozen Sets

No. 52-I—Bon Bon Bowl, Ivy Design
$24.00 per Dozen

No. 30-V—7" Diameter Plate, Open Edge, Violet Design
$26.40 per Dozen

No. 30-I—7" Diameter Plate, Open Edge, Ivy Design
$26.40 per Dozen

No. 30-R—7" Diameter Plate, Open Edge, Rose Design
$26.40 per Dozen

No. 30—Decorated with Plum, Pear, Grape and Peach
$30.00 per Dozen
(Not Illustrated)

No. 43-I—Heart Tray, Ivy Design
$14.40 per Dozen

No. 3-R—Tray, Rose Design
$18.00 per Dozen

No. 18-V—Jewel Box, Violet Design
$42.00 per Dozen

The above are available in your choice
of either Ivy, Violet or Rose Design.

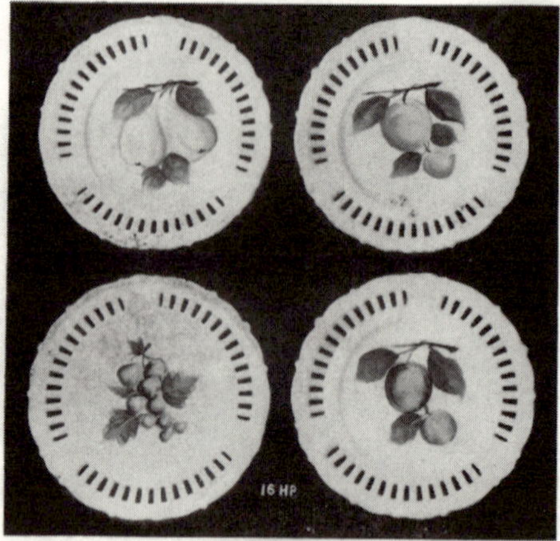

No. 16 H. P.—7" Diameter Open Edge Plate

$30.00 per Dozen

in your choice of four designs:
Pear, Peach, Grape and Plum.

No. 17 H. P.—8½" Diameter Open Edge Lovers Knot Plate

$36.00 per Dozen

in your choice of Plum, Grape, Ivy and Violet.

KEMPLE ITEM NUMBER INDEX

While compiling this index, Everett Miller found that several of Kemple's product pieces — though dissimilar — had the same item number. Those pieces were assigned the same number in different catalogs, and were manufactured at different times. This duplication is more common among the early product numbers (1-210). In a few instances, pieces originating from the same mold or belonging together in a set, would have similar item numbers, distinguishable by a letter (A, B, C, H, I, N, P, R, S or V) or a number (1, 2, 3, 4 or 5). We have selected the one or two pages for each pattern listed below on which we feel the pattern is most clearly illustrated.

Mold Abbreviations:

McK	McKee Glass Co. Purchases	MAN	Mannington Glass Co. Purchases
AMER	American Art Glass Purchases	TUSK	Tuska Purchases
SIN	Sinclair Glass Co. Purchases	Private	Private Purchase Molds
FREE	Free-hand by Kemple workers	•	Not Pictured

Item #	Pattern Name	Description	Mold	Page #
1	Hen on Nest — Split Rib Base	5¹/₂" Oval Covered Dish	McK	83
2	Scroll with Flower	Rectangular Dresser Box	MAN	60
2-A	Scroll with Flower	Stamp Box 1¹/₂" x 3¹/₂" x 1"	MAN	•
3	Scroll Variant	6" Dresser Box	MAN	16
3	Ribbed	Octagonal Ash Tray 2¹/₂" x 2¹/₂"	SIN	129
4	Scroll Variant (also #205)	9" Dresser Tray	MAN	60
4	Rooster on Nest — Split Rib Base	5¹/₂" Oval Covered Dish	McK	83
5	Scroll with Flower	Oblong Dresser Tray	MAN	12, 16
5	Pansy Flower	3-Handled Toothpick	MAN	61, 103
6	Heavy Scroll	Dresser Tray 7" x 11"	MAN	60
6	Scroll with Flower	Low Round Collar Box	MAN	16
6	Indian Chief	Match Holder	MAN	•
6-A	Scroll Variant	Oval Tray 3¹/₂"	MAN	•
7	Scroll with Fleur de Lis	Round Dresser Box	MAN	60
8	Cabbage Rose	Round Dresser Box	MAN	62
9	Lamb on Nest — Split Rib Base	5¹/₂" Oval Covered Dish	McK	83
10	Scroll Variant	Dresser Tray 7¹/₂" x 10"	MAN	60
10	Rib Base with Ash Tray Top	Oblong Combined Cigarette Box & Ash Tray	SIN	74
10	Scroll Variant	Round Covered Dresser Box	MAN	18
10-A	Plain Two Slot	Oblong Ash Tray	SIN	74
11	Lacy Heart	6" Plate	MAN	17
11	Triangle-Scroll	3-Slot Ash Tray	SIN	115
12	Fleur de Lis	Low Round Powder Box	MAN	60
12	Indian Chief	Wall Match Holder	MAN	56
12	Scroll with Fleur de Lis	8¹/₂" Oval Tray	MAN	•
13	Scroll with Fleur de Lis	Rectangular Covered Jewel Box	MAN	60
14	Sheaf of Wheat	7¹/₂" Plate	MAN	49
15	Fox on Nest — Basket Weave Base	7¹/₂" Oval Covered Dish	McK	39, 84
15	Cabbage Rose	Mug	MAN	56
16	Panel Peg — Open Edge	7¹/₂" Plate	MAN	20, 49
16-A	Sheaf of Wheat	6¹/₂" Plate	MAN	49
16-B	Lacy Heart	7¹/₂" Plate	MAN	50

Prod. #	Pattern Name	Description	Mold	Page #
17	Lovers' Knot	8¹/₂" Plate	MAN	50
18-V	Scroll with Flower	Square Covered Hankie Box	MAN	60
19-A	Mary	Plaque	MAN	56
19-B	Jesus	Plaque	MAN	56
20	Turkey on Nest — Split Rib Base	5¹/₂" Oval Covered Dish	McK	83
21	Chick	Egg Cup	MAN	62
23	Lincoln Split Rail	Oval Plaque	Private	117
24	Rooster on Nest — Basket Weave Base	7¹/₂" Oval Covered Dish	McK	84
24	Scroll Novelty	6" Oval Tray	MAN	•
25	Cat on Nest — Split Rib Base	5¹/₂" Oval Covered Dish	McK	83
25	Lady's Boot	Vase	MAN	56
26	Rabbit On Nest — Split Rib Base	5¹/₂" Oval Covered Dish	McK	83
27	Helping Hand	Ash Tray	McK	56
28	Dove on Nest — Split Rib Base	5¹/₂" Oval Covered Dish	McK	38
29	Angel Head	8¹/₂" Plate	MAN	50
30	Shell & Club	7" Plate	MAN	17, 50
30	Scroll with Fleur de Lis	Rectangular Covered Jewel Box	MAN	•
30	Diamond & Rib	Covered Dresser Box	SIN	•
31	Hen on Nest — Basket Weave Base	7¹/₂" Oval Covered Dish	McK	84
32	Puss In Boots — Pointed Toe	Slipper (Solid Sole)	MAN	61
32A	Puss In Boots — Round Toe	Slipper (Open Sole)	MAN	•
33	Cow on Nest — Basket Weave Base	7¹/₂" Oval Covered Dish	McK	39, 84
34	Duck on Nest — Split Rib Base	5¹/₂" Oval Covered Dish	McK	38
35	Lion on Nest — Basket Weave Base	7¹/₂" Oval Covered Dish	McK	84
36	Horse on Nest — Split Rib Base	5¹/₂" Oval Covered Dish	McK	83
37	Shell & Club with Waffle Face	9¹/₂" Plate	MAN	17, 50
38	Shell & Club	9¹/₂" Plate	MAN	17, 50
39	Scroll Variant	Covered Cigar Jar	MAN	60
40	Sawtooth	Candlesticks	TUSK	79
41	Sheaf of Wheat	8" Plate	MAN	49
41	Yutec	Whiskey	McK	•
42	101 — Open Edge	8¹/₂" Plate	MAN	50
43	Heart	Pin Tray	MAN	60
44	Beaded Scroll	Covered Pin Box	MAN	60
45	Hobstar & Fan	Covered Butter	McK	45
46	Sunburst	2 Handled Bon Bon	McK	75
46	Pineapple	Tall Jelly	McK	56
47	Trunk	Covered Treasure Chest	Private	62
47	Pineapple	Low Compote/Ftd. Jelly	McK	45
48	Lion Head	Rectangular Covered Dresser Box	MAN	97
49	Hobstar & Fan	Covered Footed Candy	McK	45, 78
50	Lion Head	Round Covered Dresser Box	MAN	97
50	Art Dressed	Cameo Triangular Vase	McK	93
51	Lace & Dewdrop	Covered Peanut Jar	TUSK	51
52-I	Plain Hand-Painted Ivy	6" Bowl	SIN	57
52	Ivy-in-Snow	Footed Covered Peanut Jar	TUSK	53

PROD. #	PATTERN NAME	DESCRIPTION	MOLD	PAGE #
53-V	Plain Hand-Painted Violet	Planter or Napkin Holder	SIN	136
54-V	Plain Hand-Painted Violet	Candlestick	SIN	136
54	Cabbage Rose	Oval Covered Jewel Box	MAN	60
54/1	Panel Peg with #54 Candlestick	Cake Plate	MAN	•
55-I	Plain Hand-Painted Ivy	Sugar	SIN	136
55-I	Plain Hand-Painted Ivy	Creamer	SIN	136
56	Pillar Variant	Covered Wedding Jar	McK	73
56	Aztec	Cake Plate	McK	•
57	Waffle Hat	Toothpick	MAN	•
59	Dolphin	Mustard Jar or Dish	Private	82
60	Plytec	6" Bowl	McK	•
60/2	Plytec	6" Cupped Bowl	McK	78
61	Sextec — Flower & Garland	Goblet	McK	71
62	Aztec	Footed Bon Bon	McK	64
62/C	Aztec	Crimped Footed Compote	McK	105
63	Sunburst	Celery or Ivy Vase	McK	75
64	Wedding Jar	6" Footed Covered Candy	McK	56
65	Wiltec	Footed Vase	McK	69
66	Quintec	Footed Vase	McK	34, 73
66-A	Quintec	Salt & Pepper	McK	73
67	Hobnail	Round Master Salt	Private	74
68	Carltec	6" Footed Compote	McK	68
69	Sextec — Flower & Garland	Footed Jelly	McK	33, 69
70	Toltec	Oval Footed Candlesticks	McK	79
71	Toltec	Oval Footed Nut Bowl	McK	69
72	Plytec	7" Bowl	McK	78
72/1	Plytec	7" Crimped Bowl	McK	78
72/2	Plytec	7" Rose Bowl	McK	78
72/4	Plytec	7" Banana Bowl	McK	•
73	Toast Mug	Miniature Mug	McK	62
74	Plytec	6½" Bowl	McK	34, 78
74/1	Plytec	6½" Crimped Bowl	McK	78
74/2	Plytec	6½" Rose Bowl	McK	78
75	Bontec	5" Handled Nappy	McK	67
76	Hobnail	3-Footed Candlestick	TUSK	132
77	Innovation — Medallion & Diamond	3-Toe Relish	McK	98
77-A	Bontec	Boat-Shaped Bon Bon	McK	67
78	Aztec	7" Covered Butter	McK	65
79	Valtec	5" Handled Nappy	McK	•
81	Toltec	Footed Jelly	McK	69
82	Bontec	Triangular Bon Bon	McK	67
83	Carltec	7" Oblong Bowl	McK	33, 68
84	Aztec	Creamer	McK	65
85	Aztec	Spooner	McK	65
86	Innovation — Cane Band & Rose	Napoleon's Hat Banana Boat with Base	McK	77
86-A	Innovation	Base Only	McK	•

Prod. #	Pattern Name	Description	Mold	Page #
87	Innovation — Cane Band & Rose	Napoleon's Hat Banana Boat	McK	77
88	Innovation — Canoe	13" Celery Tray	McK	75
89	Innovation — Cane Band & Rose	2-Piece Footed Compote (with #93)	McK	76
90	Ribbed	6" Square Ash Tray	SIN	74
91	Innovation — Cane Band & Rose	10" Low Bowl	McK	•
92	Innovation — V-Cane & Daisy	Oblong Pickle Dish	McK	•
93	Innovation — Cane Band & Rose	6" Compote	McK	76
94	Narcissus	Candlesticks	MAN	79
95	Yutec	9 oz. Goblet	McK	70
96	Aztec	6" Handled Nappy	McK	65
97	Yutec	Chalice	McK	58
97	Innovation — V-Cane & Daisy	$3^1/_2$ Pint Jug	McK	56
98	Valtec	Handled Heart Nappy	McK	•
99	Bontec	Handled Heart Bon Bon	McK	67
100	Innovation — V-Cane & Daisy	Footed Sherbet	McK	75
100	Ivy-in-Snow	7" Oblong Bowl	TUSK	26
101	Ivy-in-Snow	8" Oblong Bowl	TUSK	26
101	Westward Ho — Deer & Buffalo	Goblet	McK	73
101	Yutec	Footed Vase	McK	70
102	Ivy-in-Snow	9" Oblong Bowl	TUSK	26
102	Yutec	Champagne	McK	•
102-A	Yutec	3 oz. Cocktail	McK	70
103	Wiltec — Shamrock	Olive Tray	McK	35, 69
103	Ivy-in-Snow	6" Round Bowl	TUSK	•
103	Yutec	Salt Dip	McK	62
104	Ivy-in-Snow	8" Bowl	TUSK	53
104	Yutec	Champagne	McK	•
105	Ivy-in-Snow	4" Bowl	TUSK	26
105	Innovation — Sparkle	8" Bowl	McK	132
105	Yutec	2 oz. Whiskey	McK	•
106	Yutec	10" Oblong Bowl	McK	58
106	Ivy-in-Snow	5" Footed Sherbet	TUSK	26
107	Ivy-in-Snow	6" Covered Bowl	TUSK	27
107	Yutec	3 oz. Wine	McK	70
108	Yutec	Covered Sugar	McK	70
108	Ivy-in-Snow	7" Covered Candy	TUSK	27
109	Yutec	Compote	McK	58
109	Ivy-in-Snow	5" Covered Candy	TUSK	•
110	Yutec	$1^1/_2$ oz. Cordial	McK	69
110	Ivy-in-Snow	$6^1/_2$" Luncheon Plate	TUSK	53
111	Sandwich	Goblet	McK	•
111	Ivy-in-Snow	10" Plate	TUSK	53
111	Haley's Compote	Covered Compote	AMER	73
111/1	Ivy-in-Snow — Plate & Candlestick	Footed Cake Plate	TUSK	•
112	Yutec	14-Piece Punch Set	McK	58
112	Ivy-in-Snow	8" Oval Banana Split	TUSK	53
112-B	Yutec	Crimped Punch Bowl	McK	58

Prod. #	Pattern Name	Description	Mold	Page #
112-C	Yutec	Punch Cup	McK	58
113	Ivy-in-Snow	5" Saucer	TUSK	53
114	Ivy-in-Snow	3" Cup	TUSK	53
114	Innovation — Cane Panel & Daisy	6" Relish	McK	•
114-A	Innovation — Medallion & Starflower	10½" Relish	McK	•
115	Sunburst	7½" Footed Compote	McK	75
115	Ivy-in-Snow	Covered Sugar	McK	53
116	Yutec	7" Covered Butter	McK	•
116	Ivy-in-Snow	Creamer	TUSK	53
117	Yutec	10¾" Celery Tray	McK	70
117	Ivy-in-Snow	Tall Celery	TUSK	26
117/1	" "	Cup Top Vase	TUSK	26
117/2	" "	Flute Top Vase	TUSK	26
117/3	" "	6-Way Crimped Vase	TUSK	53
117/4	" "	4-Way Crimped Vase	TUSK	26
117/5	" "	Flare & Crimp Celery	TUSK	53
118	Sunburst	8½" Footed Compote	McK	75
118	Ivy-in-Snow	Boullion Cup	TUSK	27
118-A	Ivy-in-Snow	Saucer	TUSK	•
119	Yutec	7" Relish	McK	70
119	Ivy-in-Snow	Tumbler	TUSK	53
120	Ivy-in-Snow	Tall Mug	TUSK	53
121	Yutec	4½" Round Nappy	McK	58
121	Ivy-in-Snow	8 oz. Goblet	TUSK	53
122	Yutec	Toothpick	McK	70
122	Ivy-in-Snow	5 oz. Wine	TUSK	53
123	Yutec	Tumbler	McK	58
123	Ivy-in-Snow	3 oz. Wine	TUSK	•
124	Sextec — Flower & Garland	Covered Butter	McK	69
124	Ivy-in-Snow	36 oz. Water Pitcher	TUSK	53
125	Ivy-in-Snow	Candlestick	TUSK	53
126	Toltec	Celery or Vase	McK	69
126	Ivy-in-Snow	7" Bowl	TUSK	27
127	Sunburst	Footed Compote	McK	75
127	Ivy-in-Snow	Tall Celery	TUSK	26
128	Yutec	Water Pitcher	McK	58
128	Cabbage Rose	Tray 7½" x 10"	MAN	•
129	Innovation — V-Cane & Daisy	8" Nut Bowl	McK	36, 75
129	Ivy-in-Snow	Heart Nappy	TUSK	53
130	Martec	Footed Jelly	McK	33, 68
131	Wiltec	Footed Jelly	McK	69
131	Ivy-in-Snow	Covered Butter	TUSK	108
132	Small Scroll	Square Base Candlesticks	MAN	16
133	Yutec	Covered Sugar	McK	70
133	Ivy-in-Snow	8" Covered Compote	TUSK	53
134	Yutec	Condiment Tray	McK	70

Prod. #	Pattern Name	Description	Mold	Page #
134	Ivy-in-Snow	Top Hat	TUSK	•
135	Yutec	7" Low Bowl	McK	99
135	Ivy-in-Snow	10" Covered Compote	TUSK	25
136	Yutec	Covered Creamer	McK	70
137	Yutec	Salt & Pepper	McK	70
137	Ivy-in-Snow	Spooner	TUSK	•
138	Yutec	7" Round Spoon Dish	McK	•
139	Yutec	Open Sugar or Spooner	McK	70
140	Yutec	Creamer	McK	70
141	Jubilee	6" Vase	McK	37, 75
141	Ivy-in-Snow	Flare Vase	TUSK	26
142	Sunburst	Crimped Vase	McK	130
142	Ivy-in-Snow	Footed Covered Candy	TUSK	26, 53
143	Innovation — Blazier	3-Toe Bon Bon	McK	•
143	Ivy-in-Snow	Swing Vases	TUSK	27
144	Aztec	10" Vase	McK	65
145	" "	Covered Sugar or Candy	McK	65
145-C	" "	Fluted Bon Bon	McK	65
145-R	" "	Rose Bowl	McK	•
145-S	" "	Swing Vase	McK	•
146	Bontec	2-Handled Bon Bon	McK	•
147	Versailles	Rectangular Covered Cigarette Box	MAN	60
148	Innovation — Cane Panel & Daisy	Ice Tub	McK	36
149	Yutec	8-Piece Bride Set	McK	36
150	Innovation — Cane Band & Rose	4-Toe Oblong Orange Bowl	McK	76
151	Innovation — V-Cane & Daisy	12 oz. Ice Tea	McK	73
152	Innovation — V-Cane & Daisy	8 oz. Tumbler	McK	75
153	Yutec	Covered Cheese	McK	•
154	Versailles	Oval Covered Dresser Box	MAN	60
155	Versailles	Covered Dresser Box	MAN	60
156	Innovation — Cane Panel	3-Toe Round Bowl	McK	56
157	Beaded Scroll	Oval Covered Dresser Box	MAN	132
157	Scroll Variant	Low Covered Powder Jar	MAN	•
159	Sextec — Flower & Garland	Salt & Pepper	McK	69
160	Rotec	Salt & Pepper	McK	69
161	Sunburst	Salt & Pepper	McK	75
162	Basket	2-Handled Toothpick	MAN	62
163	Jubilee	8" Vase	McK	75
164	Chain Link	Cigarette Box	SIN	•
165	Plain Lid	Cigarette Box	SIN	•
166	Rotec	8" Bowl	McK	•
167	Rotec	Creamer	McK	69, 99
168	Rotec	2-Handled Sugar	McK	99
169	Champion	Condiment Holder	McK	132
170	Rotec	4" Bowl	McK	•
171	Diamond	Ice Tea Pitcher	McK	132
172	Sextec — Flower & Garland	Creamer	McK	69

PROD. #	PATTERN NAME	DESCRIPTION	MOLD	PAGE #
173	Sextec — Flower & Garland	Sugar	McK	69
174	Waffle & Button — Tappan	Child's Spooner	McK	62
175	" "	Child's Covered Sugar	McK	56, 103
176	" "	Child's Creamer	McK	56
177	" "	Child's Covered Butter	McK	56
178	Indian Chief	Toothpick	MAN	61
179	Rotec	Covered Cheese	McK	•
180	Flo	Paperweight	McK	62
180	Aztec	2 Handled Spooner	McK	•
181	Aztec	Cracker Jar	McK	65
182	Scroll Variant	8$^{1}/_{2}$" Plate	MAN	•
183	Scroll Variant	Salt Dip	MAN	•
184	Sandwich	Ice Tea	McK	78
186	" "	Tall Sherbet	McK	78
187	" "	Low Sherbet	McK	•
188	" "	Tumbler	McK	78
189	" "	Mug	McK	78
190	" "	2 Handled Open Sugar	McK	•
191	" "	Creamer	McK	78
193	Eiffel Tower — Victor	Candle Holder	McK	79
194	Rainbow	Wine	McK	56
195	Aztec	9 oz. Goblet	McK	32, 64
196	Aztec	3 oz. Wine	McK	64
197	Aztec	1 oz. Cordial	McK	64
197	Valtec	Footed Compote	McK	69
198	Panel	Finger Candlestick	McK	79
199	Beaded Scroll	7" Pin Tray	MAN	60
199	Yutec	Candlestick	McK	70
200	Wooden Tub	Master Salt	McK	46
201	Wooden Tub	Individual Salt	McK	61
201-A	Novelty Wood Tub	3" x 2$^{2}/_{3}$"	MAN	61
202	Inverted Heart — Open Edge	7" Plate	MAN	50
203	Toltec	6" Bowl	McK	32
203	Blackberry	36 oz. Pitcher	TUSK	29, 55
204	Maple Leaf — Open Edge	9" Plate	MAN	49
204A	Maple Leaf — Open Edge	6$^{1}/_{2}$" Plate	MAN	49
204	Blackberry	Goblet	TUSK	49
205	Blackberry	Creamer	TUSK	55
205	Scroll Variant (also #4)	9" Dresser Tray	MAN	•
206	Blackberry	Covered Sugar	TUSK	55
206	Pony & Cart	Ash Tray	AMER	61
207	Cabbage Leaf	7" Plate	TUSK	49
208	Toltec	Footed Toothpick	McK	69
208/1	Toltec	Swing Vase	McK	•
208	Blackberry	9" Bowl	TUSK	30
209	Lincoln Hat	Toothpick	McK	61
209	Blackberry	8" Bowl	TUSK	55

Prod. #	Pattern Name	Description	Mold	Page #
210	Coal Bucket with Bail	Ash Tray	MAN	61
210	Blackberry	7" Bowl	TUSK	•
211	Blackberry	6" Bowl	TUSK	•
212	Blackberry	5" Bowl	TUSK	55
213	Toltec	2 Handled Sugar	McK	89
213	Blackberry	4" Cereal	TUSK	•
214	Toltec	Creamer	McK	89
215	Toltec	Tall Creamer	McK	32, 56
215-A	Toltec	Tall Sugar	McK	•
216	Toltec	6" Handled Bon Bon	McK	32
217	Blackberry	Wine	TUSK	•
218	Toltec	Open Sugar	McK	•
219	Toltec	Goblet	McK	•
220	Blackberry	5" Stem Compote w/lid	TUSK	55
221	Cherub	Toothpick	McK	62
222	Toltec (also #207)	Whiskey or Toothpick	McK	131
223	Ribbed 4 Toe	Salt Dip	McK	62
224	Valtec	Creamer	McK	•
225	Valtec	Covered Sugar	McK	•
228	Diamond	Salt Dip	McK	•
239	Fish — Free Hand	Ivy Holder	FREE	73, 94
241	Bird of Paradise	Figurine	AMER	94
242	Gypsy Kettle with Slots	Ash Tray	McK	61
243	Gypsy Kettle	Toothpick	McK	61
244	Fighting Cock	Figurine	AMER	81
245	Basket Weave	Toothpick	MAN	61
246	Banzantine	Fan Vase	McK	•
247	" "	Creamer	McK	•
247-A	" "	Sugar	McK	73
248	" "	Sherbet	McK	•
249	Rex Variant	Mustard Jar with Cover	McK	73
250	Sandwich Basket	8" Plate	MAN	•
251	Deer (Llama)	Figurine	AMER	81
252	Pheasant	Figurine	AMER	81
253	Jumping Horse	Figurine	AMER	81
254	Grouse	Figurine	AMER	81
255	Stage Coach	Figurine	AMER	94
256	Southern Belle with Hat	Figurine	AMER	56, 114
257	Colonial Lady with Basket	Figurine	AMER	56, 114
258	Victorian Lady	Figurine	AMER	56, 114
259-A	Dutch Boy	Book End	AMER	56
259-B	Dutch Girl	Book End	AMER	56
260-A	Caesar	Egyptian Ash Tray	AMER	74
260-B	Cleopatra	Egyptian Ash Tray	AMER	74
261	Horse	Ash Tray	AMER	•
262	Indian	Ash Tray	AMER	62
263	Crucifix — Floral Base	7½" Candlestick	MAN	79

Prod. #	Pattern Name	Description	Mold	Page #
264-A	Crucifix — Bell Base	10" Candlestick	McK	79
265	Hatchet	Figurine	McK	62
266	Diamond Shell	Mustard Spoon	McK	82
267	Easter Egg	6" x 5" Whimsey	MAN	62
268	Easter Egg	4" x 5" Whimsey	MAN	•
269	Swan	Vase (5 Sizes)	FREE	•
270	Scroll with Beaded Edge	Salt Dip	MAN	•
271	Loving Cup	3-Handled 4" x 26"	McK	•
272	Star with Tear Drops	Ash Tray	McK	74
273	Spade	5" Ash Tray	MAN	•
274	Heart, Spade, Club, Diamond	4 pc. 3" Playing Card Ash Tray	MAN	74
275	Cherub Plaque	10" x 6" Plaque	MAN	73
276	Scroll Variant	Round Toothpick	MAN	89
277	Scroll Variant	Square Toothpick	MAN	62
278	Scroll Variant	Hex Toothpick	MAN	62
279	Carltec	2-Handled Bon Bon	McK	•
280	Scroll Variant	4" Match Holder	MAN	•
282	Innovation — V- Cane & Daisy	Toothpick	McK	62
283	Horseshoe	Pen Holder	McK	46
284	Church	Figurine (Lamp)	AMER	94
285	Lion	Pin Tray 4$\frac{1}{2}$" x 2$\frac{1}{2}$"	MAN	•
286	Shell	3-Toe 6" Ash Tray	McK	•
287	Puritan	Whiskey	McK	•
288	Shell	Salt Dip	McK	56
289	Horseshoe	Ash Tray	MAN	•
290	Unidentified	Ash Tray with Lighter Holder		•
291	Innovation — Daisy with Scallop Edge	$\frac{1}{4}$ lb. Butter Dish	McK	•
292	Leaning Ash Tray	Ash Tray	AMER	73
293	Banzantine	6" Footed Bowl	McK	•
294	" "	Candlestick	McK	•
295	" "	Small Mug	McK	•
296	" "	6" Scallop Compote	McK	•
297	Table Lamp	Table Lamp	Private	93
298	Lamp Base	Lamp Base	Private	57, 93
299	Lamp Base	Lamp Base	Private	93
300	Moon & Star Variant	8" Bowl	TUSK	29
301	" "	10" Bowl	TUSK	54
301-A	" "	12" Cake Plate	TUSK	54
302	" "	11" Flute Bowl	TUSK	29
303	" "	12" Low Banana Boat	TUSK	54
304	" "	Candlesticks	TUSK	28, 54
305	" "	11" Crimped Bowl	TUSK	54
306	" "	Compote on Candlestick	TUSK	54
307	" "	Footed Compote	TUSK	54
308	" "	Footed Banana Boat	TUSK	28, 54
309	" "	11" Footed Cake Stand	TUSK	69

Prod. #	Pattern Name	Description	Mold	Page #
500	Toltec	Blown Vase with Ruffled Mouth	McK	59
501	" "	Ewer with Crimped Spout	McK	•
502	" "	Pitcher	McK	59
503	" "	Bottle with Stopper	McK	•
504	" "	Decanter with Stopper	McK	•
505	Rib Base	Ewer with Ruffled Spout	McK	43
505-H	" "	Ewer with Ruffled Spout	McK	•
506	" "	Vase with Rigaree	McK	43
506-S	" "	Vase with Ruffled Mouth	McK	•
507	" "	Ewer with Elongated Spout	McK	43
507-T	" "	Ewer with Elongated Spout	McK	•
508	" "	Decanter with Stopper and Handle	McK	43, 85
509	" "	Bottle with Stopper	McK	43
510	Rainbow	Ewer with Ruffled Spout	McK	43
511	" "	Decanter	McK	59
511/1	" "	Vase with Large Mouth	McK	85
512	" "	Ewer with Tipped Spout	McK	59
513	" "	Bottle with Stopper	McK	85
514	" "	Ewer with Stopper	McK	43
515	Lacey Heart	Vase with Rigaree	McK	85
515-N	Lacey Heart	Vase with Large Mouth	McK	59
516	Lacey Heart	Ewer with Crimped Spout	McK	59
518	Optic	Ewer with Tipped Spout	McK	59
518	Lacey Heart	Ewer with Tipped Spout	McK	40
519	Lacey Heart	Bottle with Stopper	McK	40
520	Lacey Heart	Decanter with Stopper	McK	40
521	Plutec	Ewer with Ruffled Spout	McK	•
522	" "	Vase	McK	59
523	" "	Ewer with Elongated Spout	McK	•
524	" "	Bottle with Stopper	McK	34
525	" "	Decanter with Stopper	McK	•
526	Champion	Cruet with Stopper	McK	86
528	" "	Vase with Ruffled Mouth	McK	85
528/1	" "	Wide Mouth Vase	McK	86
529	" "	Ewer with Crimped Spout	McK	86
530	Panel	Vase with Rigaree	McK	•
530-S	" "	Vase with Rigaree	McK	•
531	" "	Ewer with Spout	McK	•
531-H	" "	Ewer with Spout	McK	•
532	" "	Ewer with Elongated Spout	McK	•
532-T	" "	Ewer with Elongated Spout	McK	•
533	" "	Decanter with Stopper	McK	•
533	Rose Pattern	9$^{1}/_{2}$" Plate	MAN	•
534	Panel	Cruet	McK	59
535	Natural Crackle	Ewer with Stopper	McK	85
535-H	Natural Crackle	Ewer with Ruffled Spout	McK	•
536	Natural Crackle	Vase	McK	•

Prod. #	Pattern Name	Description	Mold	Page #
536-SV	Natural Crackle	Vase	McK	•
537	" "	Ewer with Tipped Spout	McK	•
538	" "	Decanter with Stopper	McK	•
539	" "	Bottle with Stopper	McK	•
540-H	Panel — Serrated Neck	Ewer with Crimped Spout	McK	•
541/5	Panel — Serrated Neck	Vase	McK	•
543	Panel	Bottle with Stopper	McK	•
544	Panel	Decanter with Stopper	McK	•
545	Optic	Vase with Ruffled Mouth	McK	•
546	Optic	Bulbous Vase	McK	•
547	Optic	Pitcher	McK	•
548	Natural Crackle	Ewer with Ruffled Spout	McK	40
549	" "	Vase with Rigaree	McK	40
550	" "	Decanter with Handle	McK	86
551	" "	Bulbous Decanter with Spout	McK	•
552	Champion Petticoat	3 Bottles & Toothpick	McK	132
553	Natural Crackle	Bulbous Pitcher	McK	85, 86
555	Optic	Bulbous Vase with Rigaree	McK	85
556	Optic	Vase with Snake on Neck	McK	41
557	Natural Crackle	Bottle with Stopper	McK	•
558	Optic	Ewer with Elongated Spout	McK	41
560	" "	Tall Vase	McK	•
561	" "	Tall Vase with Leaf	McK	85
562	" "	Tall Pitcher	McK	•
562-A	" "	Vase	McK	•
563	" "	Flare Vase with Leaf	McK	•
564	" "	Tankard Pitcher	McK	•
565	Optic Swirl	Ruffle Top Vase	McK	•
566	Optic Swirl	Vase	McK	•
567	Pinched Optic	Ewer with Crimped Spout	McK	•
568	Pinched Optic	Bulbous Decanter	McK	86
570	Pinched Optic	Bulbous Vase	McK	•
571-HS	Optic	Decanter with Stopper	McK	86
572-SS	" "	Bottle with Stopper	McK	•
573-H	" "	Ewer with Crimped Spout	McK	85
574-P	" "	Ewer	McK	•
575-SS	" "	Bottle with Snake on Neck	McK	•
576-H	Pinched Optic	Ewer with Crimped Top	McK	•
578-S	Optic	Vase with Rigaree	McK	85
579	" "	Tall Bottle with Stopper	McK	•
580-SS	" "	Bottle with Snake on Neck	McK	•
581	" "	Vase with Ruffle Top	McK	86
582	" "	Bulbous Pitcher	McK	•
583	" "	Bulbous Vase with Leaf	McK	•
585	Panel	Pitcher	McK	42
587	Panel	Flute Vase	McK	•
589	Optic	Bulbous Pitcher	McK	40

Prod. #	Pattern Name	Description	Mold	Page #
590	Optic	Vase with Rigaree	McK	41
592-P	" "	Flare Vase	McK	•
593	" "	Cruet	McK	•
594	" "	Ewer	McK	•
595	" "	Tall Flare Pitcher	McK	•
595-P	" "	Unidentified	McK	•
595-ST	" "	Unidentified	McK	•
596	" "	Tall Flare Vase	McK	85
596-P	" "	Tall Flare Vase	McK	•
596-SY	" "	Tall Flare Vase	McK	•
597	" "	3" High Plain Top Creamer	McK	•
598	" "	3" High Plain Top Sugar	McK	•
599	" "	Large Mouth Vase	McK	•
600	Natural Crackle	Bulbous Vase	McK	•
601	Optic	Pitcher	McK	•
602-HS	" "	Decanter with Stopper	McK	•
603-ST	" "	Bottle	McK	•
603-SS	" "	Bottle with Stopper	McK	85
604	" "	Bulbous Vase	McK	•
604-SV	" "	Bulbous Wide Mouth Vase	McK	•
605	Swirl	Vase with Ruffled Mouth	McK	42
606	Swirl	Ewer with Handle	McK	42
608	Natural Crackle	Vase with Ruffled Mouth	McK	•
609	Optic	Pitcher	McK	41
612	Panel	Bulbous Vase with Rigaree	McK	42
613	" "	Ewer with Handle and Ruffled Spout	McK	42
614	" "	Decanter with Stopper	McK	42
615	" "	Vase	McK	•
615-S	" "	Vase with Snake on Neck	McK	•
616	" "	Ewer	McK	•
617	Optic	Bottle with Snake on Neck	McK	•
618	" "	Ewer with Crimped Spout	McK	•
619-SY	" "	Flare Vase	McK	•
620-P	" "	Pitcher	McK	•
621	Optic Swirl	Vase with Ruffled Mouth	McK	•
622	" "	Flare Top Vase	McK	85
623	" "	Crimped Top Slender Pitcher	McK	•
624	" "	Slender Pitcher	McK	39
625	Yutec	Ewer with Handle	McK	85
626	Yutec	Decanter with Stopper	McK	59
627	Yutec	Cruet	McK	73
628	Toltec	Mug	McK	•
629	Natural Crackle	Ewer	McK	•
630	Optic	Mug	McK	•
632	Panel Variant	5" Ewer	McK	•
633	Panel Variant	5" Cruet	McK	•
634	Natural Crackle	Ewer	McK	•

Prod. #	Pattern Name	Description	Mold	Page #
635	Optic	Sugar	McK	62
636	Optic	Creamer	McK	62
638	Natural Crackle (also #551)	Decanter with Rigaree	McK	40
639	Natural Crackle	Pitcher	McK	86
640	Optic	Vase	McK	•
641	Optic	Cruet	McK	57
649	Sunburn	Ewer	McK	44
650	" "	Vase	McK	•
651	" "	Cruet with Stopper	McK	85, 86
652	" "	Decanter with Stopper	McK	44
653	Yutec	Vase with Rigaree	McK	35
654	Yutec	Bottle with Stopper	McK	35
656	Yutec	Ship Decanter	McK	59
660	Sunburst	Vase	McK	34
661	" "	Ewer with Slant Neck/Lazy Joe	McK	34
662	" "	Bottle with Stopper	McK	34
663	" "	Ewer	McK	34
664	" "	Ewer with Stopper	McK	34
665	" "	Cruet	McK	•
666	" "	Creamer	McK	•
670	Optic	Bottle with Stopper	McK	•
901	Lion Head	Dresser Tray 7" x 11"	MAN	18
911	Scroll with Flower	Glove Box 4" x 12"	MAN	•
966	Plytec	3" x 6" Bowl	McK	•
971	Scroll Variant	Octagonal Tobacco Jar	MAN	•
973	Open Edge	Square Cup	SIN	•
974	Open Edge	Square Saucer	SIN	•
975	Open Edge	8" Square Plate	SIN	49, 115
993	Mary & Child	6" Plate	MAN	62
1018	Loving Cup	6" Vase	McK	•
1035	Scroll Variant	3" x 3" Square Pin Box	MAN	•

KEMPLE PATTERN NAME INDEX

This index lists Kemple pattern names and the pages on which they are discussed and/or illustrated. To avoid confusion, only Kemple products are included—not Wheaton reproductions.

NOTES

Everett Miller's research made us aware of other existing Kemple patterns. We have listed them below but because of inadequate catalog or photo references of these patterns, they do not appear in the Pattern Name Index or elsewhere in the book.

Innovation Cut—Blazier
Innovation Cut—Cand Band & Daisy
Cherub (plaque)
Daisy with Scalloped Edge
Loving Cup
Medallion & Star Flower
Plain Lid
Puritan
Ribbed Four-Toe
Spade

KEMPLE GLASS: 1945 - 1970
1997 - 1998 VALUE GUIDE

The first section of this guide prices nearly 800 items pictured in color on pages 49-94. The second section assigns values to hundreds of other pieces from the catalog reprints on pages 95-112. Many items appear in both sections. In such cases, identical items should have the same value. Variations in color may account for some price differences. When a value range rather than a single price appears, this usually refers to price differences on the basis of color. See the NOTES section at the end of this guide for more specific information.

Section One lists the figure number for each piece as it appears in the photograph and caption. A suggested retail price follows. Section Two identifies the catalog items by page number (in this book) and product number as shown in the reprint. To make identification possible, numbers have been assigned to pieces in those reprints that do not have product numbers.

Wheatonware and Wheatoncraft products are valued below comparable Kemple items for two reasons: the Wheaton products are newer and, in our judgment, they lack the pattern detail, clarity of color, and overall quality of the Kemple wares.

Prices are for items in mint condition (sold retail) without chips, cracks or other defects. Decorated articles should be free of blemishes in the hand painting. Pieces vary in price according to their color. Amethyst or Amberina will be slightly higher than more common colors—milk glass, blue, green, or amber; End-of-Day higher still; West Virginia Red even higher; and any Gray assortment will be priced highest because of its rarity.

Kemple values are less firmly established than prices for glass made by larger, better-known companies. Although we've tried to produce a fair, realistic guide, prices in the field will vary considerably. In a few cases, pieces are not priced (N/P), usually because of extreme rarity. Finally, we need to issue our standard disclaimer: the publisher and authors cannot accept responsibility or liability for losses incurred by persons using this guide, whether due to typographical errors or other reasons.

Figure	Value	Figure	Value	Figure	Value	Figure	Value	Figure	Value
1	$ 25	19	$ 20	37	$ 45	52	$ 18	70	$ 20
2	15	20	25	38	45 ea.	53	20	71	30
3	15	21	25		80 pr.	54	25	72	20
4	25	22	25	39	15	55	12	73	20
5	25	23	25	40	15 ea.	56	65	74	50
6	25	24	25		25 pr.	57	15	72-74	75
7	15	25	25	41	20	58	15	75	10
8	20	26	35	42	18	59	15	76	12
9	20	27	25	44	18 ea.	60	20	77	15
10	20	28	25		35 pr.	61	18	78	12
11	20	29	30	43	55	62	15	79	20
12	20	30	65	45	12	63	20	80-81	45 ea.,
13	30	31	45	46	18	64	30		50 pr.
14	25	32	35	47	20	65	70	82	12
15	25	33	55	48	30	66	25	83	15
16	25	34	25	49	18 set	67	25	84	18
17	25	35	25	50	65	68	65	85	12
18	25	36	45	51	20	69	16 set	86	35

Figure	Value	Figure	Value	Figure	Value	Figure	Value	Figure	Value
87	$ 70	134	$ 45	187	$ 30	278	$ 25	347	$ 12
88	35	135	10	188	30	279	20	348	15
86-88	90	136	20	189	45	280	35	349	15
89	35	137	20	190	35	281	20	350-351	45 ea.
90	35	138	35	191	45	282	80	352	55
91	25	139	25	192	65	283	20	353	15-20
92	45	140	65	193	35	284	20	354	15
93	25	141	38	194	35	285	35	355-357	15-20
91-93	65	142	35	195	45	286	20	358	35
94	35	143	45	196-197	35 ea.	287	35	359	20
95	16	144	30	198	15	288	20	360	25
96	35	145	55	199	20	289	20	361	20
97	30	146	30	200	18	290-291	20 ea.	358-361	80
98	35	147	25	201	18	292	15	362	55
99	85	148	30	202	20	293-296	25 ea.	363	45
100	100	149	25	203	15	297	15	364	15-20
101	80	150	22	204	15	298	15	365	45
102	150	151	22	205-206	22 ea.	299-300	15 ea.	366	15
103	55	152	25	207	18	301	45	367-369	15-20
104	55	153-155	15 ea.	208	18	302	55	370-374	18-20
105	55	156	22	209	18	303	55	375-378	18-20
106	55	157	18	210-212	15 ea.	304	55	379	18
105-106	100	158-160	20 ea.	213	18	305	45	380	18
107	55	161	12	214	18	306	45	381	18
108	65	162	15	215	20	307	20	382	18
109	65	163-164	15 ea.	216	18	308	18	383-385	18
110	55	165	30	217	22	309-310	8 ea.	386-390	35-45
111	45	166	30	218	28	311	18	391	18
112	60	167	65	219	55 set	312-314	20 ea.	392	15
113-114	45 ea.	168	22	220	22	315	18	393-394	18 ea.
115	40	169	45	221	55 set	316-318	15 ea.	395-400	15-45,
116-117	45 ea.	170	18	222-226	22 ea.	319-321	2 ea.		(WV Red—145)
118	75	171	75	227-231	25 ea.	322-323	12 ea.	401	30 pr.
119	25	172	22	232-237	35 ea.	324	12	402	35
120	65	173	35	238-241	35 ea.	325	25	403	30 pr.
121	64	174	45	242-247	45	326	35	404	35
122	85	175	275	248-252	25 ea.	327	32	405	18
123	45	176	45	253-260	25 ea.	328	N/P	406	30
124	65	177	30	261-265	25 ea.	329	25	407	18
125	65	178	30	266-268	18	330	25	408-410	20
126	65	179	30	269-270	15	331	25	411	17 set
127-128	40 ea.,	180	65	271	25	332	30	412	35
	75 set	181	85	272	20	333	25	413	35
129	35	182	55	273	20	334	25	414-415	18
130	35	183	45	274	35	335	25	416	25
131-132	45 ea.,	184	35	275	20	336	25	417-418	35 pr.
	80 pr.	185	35	276	20	337-345	28-40	419	18
133	65	186	35	277	35	346	15	420-421	45 pr.

Figure	Value	Figure	Value	Figure	Value	Figure	Value	Figure	Value
422	$ 15	475	$ 75	532	$ 25	602	$ 30	653	$ 65
423	20	476	25	533	25	603	45	654	65
424	12	477	175	534-535	35 ea.	604	25	655	55
425	18	478	150	536-539	125	605	28	656	60
426	17 pr.	479	65	(base only, 35 ea.)		606	15	657	45
427	18	480	18	540	75	607	17	658	65
428	75	481	20	541-545	95-250	608	28	659	75
429	15	482	25	546	25	609	40	660	38
430	20	483	175	547	30	610	35	661	30
431	20	484	75	548	35	611-615	12	662	50
432	22	485	75	549-553	45-55	616	18	663	50
433	35	486	20	554	18	617	45 ea.,	664	55
434	45	487	85	555	15		80 pr.	665	25
435	35	488	45	556	15	618	45	666	45
436	22	489	45	557	18	619-620	40 ea.,	667	35
437	18 pr.	490	35	558	20		70 pr.	668	35
438	35	491	35	559	15	621-622	45 ea.,	669	55
439	35	492	25	560	14		80 pr.	670	45
440	35	493	25	561	14	623	45	671	45
441	12	494	20 pr.	562	12	624	85	672	35
442	20	495	20	563	18	625	120	673	18
443	35	496	65	564	18	626	85	674	38
444	35	497-501	35 ea.	565	15	627	115	675	10
445	12	502-503	45 ea.,	566	20	628	115	676	35
446	25		85 pr.	567	25	629	95	677	65
447	18	504	20	568	45	630	95	678	45
448	12	505	25	569	35	631	275	679	55
449	45	506	20	570-571	20 ea.,	632	325	680	55
450	18	507	15 ea.		35 pr.	633	85	681	55
451	20	508	35	572-580	25-35	634	115	682	55
452	18	509	20		(pr., 45-60)	635	85	683	45
453	23	510	25	581-585	20-25	636	85	684	55
454	20	511	25		(pr., 35-45)	637	15	685	55
455	18	512	32	586-588	20 ea.,	638	45	686	35
456	20	513	45		35 pr.	639	60	687	55
457	20	514	25	589-590	20 ea.,	640	60	688	55
458	23	515-518	15 ea.,		35 pr.	641	45	689	45
459	30		40 set	591	20	642	60	690	35
460	55-65	519	28	592	42	643	55	691	35
461	40	520	35	593	40	644	65	692	30
462	65	521	45	594	40	645	45	693-694	35 ea.
463	18	522	18	595	14	646	45	695	35
464	18	523	25	596	45	647	85	696	45
465-466	18 ea.	524	20	597	14	648	85	697	35
467-471	20-35	525	35	598	40	649	65	698	35
472	20	526-528	35 ea.	599	30	650	100	699	45
473	65	529-530	18 ea.	600	45	651	65	700	35
474	18	531	18 pr.	601	30	652	65	701	35

Figure	Value	Figure	Value	Figure	Value	Figure	Value	Figure	Value
702	$ 345 set	720	$ 85	741	$ 250	759	$ 225	780	$ 375
703	75	721	275	742	225	760	65	781	110
704	40	722-723	165 pr.	743	275	761	85	782	110
705	250	724	95	744	125	762	45	783	90
706	75	725-726	70 pr.	745	125	763-764	125 pr.	784	90
707	275	727	85	746	275	765	65	785	75
708-709	190 set	728	225	747	125	766	85	786	175
710	85	729	55	748	85	767	145	787	250
711	125	730	275	749	85	768	145	788	85
712	125	731	225	750	75	769	55	789	85
713	135	732	225	751	85	770	325	790	85
714	85	733	65	752	75	771-773	185 set	791	450
715	75	734	225	753	125	774	55	792	350
716	75	735	65	754	225	775	65	793	450
717	365 hat	736	225	755	225	776	85	794	135
	85 base	737	125	756	225	777	95	795	125
718	185	738	85	757	225	778	375	796	90
719	95	739-740	185 set	758	85	779	375		

SECTION TWO: CATALOG PAGE REPRINTS

The following section identifies the catalog items by *page number* (in this book) and *product number* as shown in the reprint. Numbers have been assigned to pieces in those reprints that do not have product numbers.

Wheatonware and Wheatoncraft products are valued lower than Kemple items because they are newer and, in our judgment, they lack the pattern detail, clarity of color, and overall quality of the Kemple wares.

Figure	Value	Figure	Value	Figure	Value	Figure	Value	Figure	Value
PG. 95		GR49	$ 55	**PG. 97**		408	$ 20-35	20	$ 225
FR40	$ 25-35	GR69	20	115	$ 35	94	35 pr.	103	12
	(pr., 45-60)	GR63	30-40	97	275	31	65	32	35
FR68	35-45	GR130	18	244	40	133	35	89	125
FR115	35	GR40	35 ea.,	29	35	136	35		
FR97	275		60 pr.	409	65	70	45-60	**PG. 99**	
FR197	20	GR66	24	72/C	125		(pr.)	E62	95
FR62	95	GR197	24	4	225			B70	35 pr.,
FR145	25	GR408	20-35	78	35	**PG. 98**			20 ea.
ED93	85	GR70	60 pr.	137	75	66	20	G86	175
ED49	45-55	GR93	85	402	45	49	45	B70	35 pr.,
ED81	85	GR139, 140	190 set	8	22	159	17 set		20 ea.
ED4	225	GR68	45	48	35	59	325	B46	25
ED59	325	GR208	12	50	35	152	18	84	20
ED36	225	GR145	25-30	208	12	77	18	85	20
ED20	225	GR72/1	150	197	20	5	35	B159	17 set
		GR410	24	130	15	83	18	B173	17.50
PG. 96		GR72	150	18	28	133	35	B172	17.50
GR62	95	GR71	N/P	86	95-250	151	22	B168	17.50

Figure	Value
B167	$ 17.50
E199	20 ea.
B94	20 ea., 35 pr.
E74	20
E198	15
G88	35
B135	20
G99	18
B83	18

PG. 100

Figure	Value
AM197	12-15
197	12-15
B197	12-15
G197	12-15
G69	18
69	18
B93	85
93	85
G93	85
B130	145
AM130	145
AM69	18
B69	18
AM49	55
49	45
B49	45
G49	45
130	145
G130	145
G133 (sold with No. 136)	165
AM133 (sold with No. 136)	165
G145	125
AM145	125
B133 (sold with No. 136)	165
133 (sold with No. 136)	165
G97	65
B97	65
97	65
AM97	65
145	125
B145	125

PG. 101

Figure	Value
AM4	$ 45
B4	45
4	45
G4	45
G25	55
25	55
B25	55
AM25	55
AM9	45
B9	45
9	45
G9	45
G1	45
1	45
B1	45
AM1	45
AM36	65
B36	65
36	65
G36	65
G20	60
20	60
B20	60
AM20	60

PG. 102

Figure	Value
89	125
E101	75
G61	20
B195	15
G118	45
B33	100
G35	65
B15	65
G24	65
B31	65
E129	35
B100	18
G134	35
B117	22
G90	35
408	20
409	56
E159	17 set
160	17 pr.
G137	18 pr.

Figure	Value
B108	$ 45
71	15
B123	18
B128	75

PG. 103

Figure	Value
AM122	12
122	12
B122	12
G122	12
AM206	25
206	25
B206	25
G206	25
G178	45
B178	45
178	45
AM178	45
G5	35
B5	35
5	35
AM5	35
AM175	25
175	25
B175	25
G175	25
AM32	35
B32	35
G32	35
G210	22
B210	22
210	22
AM210	22
G176	20
176	20
AM176	20
AM245	25
245	25
B245	25
G245	25
AM208	12
208	12
B208	12
G208	12
G67	15
B67	15
67	15

Figure	Value
AM67	$ 15
B242	25
242	25
AM242	25

PG. 104

Figure	Value
B40	25
40	25
T115	35
115	35
G115	35
G40	25
AM40	25
G59	275
B59	275
59	275
AM59	275
AM78	80
B78	80
78	80
G78	80
G124	35
124	35
B124	35
AM124	35
G139, 140	190 set
AM103	18
G103	18
82	18
B82	18
133 (sold with No. 136)	165
136 (sold with No. 133)	165
B103	18
103	18
AM82	18
G82	18
B133 (sold with No. 136)	165
B136 (sold with No. 133)	165

PG. 105

Figure	Value
62/C	15-20
69	18
93	85

Figure	Value
145	$ 125
145/C	15-20
206	25
121	22
245/243	25
117	22
1	45
25	55
16	25
99	18
122	12
40	25
61	23
82	18
160	17 pr.
111	75
415	55-65
129	35
67	15
75	18
106	35

PG.106

Figure	Value
1	26
2	34
3	15-16
4	11
5	26
6	20 pr.
7	20 pr.
8	34
9	26
10	15 ea.
11	15 ea.
12	12 ea.
13	12 ea.
14	26 pr.
15	26 pr.
16	N/P
17	15 ea.
18	15 ea.
A	15-16
B	75
C	26
D	64 pr.
E	52
F	14

Figure	Value	Figure	Value	Figure	Value	Figure	Value	Figure	Value
G	$ 26	J	$ 26	288	$ 10	204	$ 26	**PG.112**	
H	52	K	56 set	290	12 pr.	172	94	290	$ 26 pr.
I	52	L	82	272	16	192	26	276	49
J	15		(with spoon)	268	9	170	20	258	10
K	56 set	M	26	282	41	152	11	252	14
L	82 set	N	15	278	38 set			250	22
M	14	O	11	280	36	**PG.111**		254, 256	14 set
N	34-41	P	64 pr.	252	14	214	N/P	284	49
O	26	Q	14	258	12	764	16	282	41
P	26	R	34-41	250	22	768	28	296	41
Q	11	S	14	254, 256	14 set	216	20 pr.	286	34
R	94	1	41			212	15 ea.	272	16
S	N/P	2	15-16	**PG.109**		744	41	268	9
T	N/P	3	15	296	41	158, 159	82 set	280	36
		4	15	184	N/P	194	12	278	38 set
		5	15	198	15-16	210	12 ea.	288	10
PG.107		6	52			290	12 pr.		
A	52	7	52	**PG.110**		174	14		
B	52	8	52	154	75	188	28		
C	52			202	26	190	28		
D	26			156	67	178, 180 &			
E	75	**PG.108**		150	34-41	182	56 set		
F	15-16	296	41	206	26	218	26 pr.		
G	32	284	49	196	26				
H	32	276	49	176	15				
I	41	286	34						

NOTES

Figures 337-345 are valued at $28 each in milk glass, blue, and amber; in amberina, vaseline, amethyst and green, they are valued at $40 each.

Figure 353 is valued at $15 in miscellaneous colors; in amberina, it is slightly higher at $20.

Figures 355-357 are valued at $15 in miscellaneous colors; in amberina, it is slightly higher at $20.

Figure 364 in miscellaneous colors is valued at $15, and in amberina, at $20.

Figures 367-369 in miscellaneous colors are valued at $15 each, and in amberina, $20 each.

Figures 370-374 are valued at $18 each in miscellaneous colors, and $20 in amberina or dark amethyst.

Figures 395-400 are valued at $15 each in miscellaneous colors, $45 in dark amethyst or amberina, and $145 in the 1963 West Virginia Red.

Figures 541-545 are valued according to the following: $175 each for the 2-pc. set, or $95 each for just the bowl; $250 for the set in amberina and dark amethyst; $200 for the set in dark green.

Figures 549-553 are valued at $45 each in miscellaneous colors; and $55 in dark amethyst, dark green or amberina.

Figures 572-580 are valued at $25 each or $45 for a pair, in miscellaneous colors; in dark amethyst and amberina, they are valued at $35 each or $60 for a pair.

Figures 581-585 are valued at $20 each or $35 a pair; in dark amethyst and amberina, they are valued at $25 each or $45 a pair.

PG.95 ED49 is valued at $45 each in miscellaneous colors; and $55 in dark amethyst, dark green or amberina.

PG.95 FR40 is valued at $25 each or $45 for a pair, in miscellaneous colors; in dark amethyst and amberina, valued at $35 each or $60 for a pair.

PG.97 86 and **PG.99 G86** are valued according to the following: $175 each for the 2-pc. set, or $95 each for just the bowl; $250 for the set in amberina and dark amethyst; $200 for the set in dark green.

PG.97 70 is valued at $20 each or $35 a pair; in dark amethyst and amberina, valued at $25 each or $45 a pair.

BIBLIOGRAPHY

Allison, Grace. "Artisan John Kemple—His Exquisite Glass." *Tri-State Trader*, Vol. 8, No. 43 (January 31, 1976), Knightstown, IN, pp. 1-3.

Allison, Grace. "Kemple Glass." *Glass Review*, May 1985.

Belknap, E. McCamly. *Milk Glass*. New York: Crown Publishers, 1959.

Buckley, Don E. "Glass by Gas." *The East Ohio News*, c.1950.

Editor. "Glass-Making at Kenova." *Norfolk and Western Magazine*, November 1958.

Ferson, Regis F. and Mary F. *Yesterday's Milk Glass Today*. Self published, 1981.

Field, Zane. "Many Items From Kemple Glass Co. Were Reproduced in Original Molds." *Collector's Weekly*, Vol. 3, No. 114 (November 23, 1971), Kermit, TX, pp. 1-2.

Grist, Everett. *Covered Animal Dishes*. Paducah, KY: Collector Books, no date.

Husfloen, Kyle. *Collector's Guide to American Pressed Glass, 1825-1915*. Radnor, PA: Wallace-Homestead Book Company, 1992.

Innes, Lowell. *Pittsburgh Glass, 1797-1891*. Boston: Houghton Mifflin Company, 1976.

Innes, Lowell and Jane Shadel Spillman. *M'Kee Victorian Glass, Five Complete Glass Catalogs from 1859/60 to 1871*. New York: Dover Publications, Inc., 1981.

Jenks, Bill and Jerry Luna. *Early American Pattern Glass 1850-1910*. Radnor, PA: Wallace-Homestead Book Company, 1990.

Jenks, Bill, Jerry Luna and Darryl Reilly. *Identifying Pattern Glass Reproductions*. Radnor, PA: Wallace-Homestead Book Company, 1993.

Kemple advertisement. *China & Glass Red Book*, 1949.

Kemple advertisement. *Crockery & Glass Journal*, April 1950.

Kemple news feature. *East Palestine (Ohio) Daily Leader*, April 10, 1951.

McCorkhill, Georgia. "Antiques and Hobbies." *Farm and Dairy* (Salem, Ohio), September 26, 1948.

Measell, James. *Greentown Glass: The Indiana Tumbler & Goblet Company*. Grand Rapids, MI: Grand Rapids Public Museum, 1979.

Metz, Alice Hulett. *Early American Pattern Glass*. Paducah, KY: Collector Books, 1978.

Metz, Alice Hulett. *Much More Early American Pattern Glass*. Paducah, KY: Collector Books, 1978.

Millard, S.T. *Opaque Glass*. Topeka, KS: Central Press, 1953.

Lee, Ruth Webb. *Victorian Glass*. Wellesley Hills, MA: Lee Publications, 1944.

Revi, Albert Christian. *American Pressed Glass and Figure Bottles*. New York: Thomas Nelson Inc., 1964.

Shumpert, Gwen. "Kemple Glass." *Rainbow Review Glass Journal*, December 1974.

Stout, Sandra McPhee. *The Complete Book of McKee Glass*. North Kansas City: The Trojan Press, 1972.

Taylor, Gay LeCleire. Unpublished Lecture Notes on Kemple Molds. Millville, NJ: Museum of American Glass, c.1991.

Warman, Edwin G. *Milk Glass Addenda*. Uniontown, PA: E.G. Warman Publishing Co., 1966.

Welker, John & Elizabeth. *Pressed Glass in America., Encyclopedia of the First Hundred Years, 1825-1925*. Doylestown, PA: Antique Acres Press, 1985.

Wilson, Jack D. *Phoenix & Consolidated Art Glass, 1926-1980*. Marietta, OH: Antique Publications, 1989.

Wilson, Kenneth M. *American Glass, 1760-1930*, Vol. I and II. New York: Hudson Hills Press, 1994.